Your Family, Inc.
Practical Tips for Building a Healthy Family Business

Your Family, Inc.
Practical Tips for Building a Healthy Family Business

Ellen Frankenberg, PhD

Routledge
Taylor & Francis Group
New York London

First published by

The Haworth Mental Health Press, an imprint of The Haworth Press, Inc., 10 Alice Street, Binghamton, NY 13904-1580

This edition published 2012 by Routledge

Routledge
Taylor & Francis Group
711 Third Avenue
New York, NY 10017

Routledge
Taylor & Francis Group
2 Park Square, Milton Park
Abingdon, Oxon OX14 4RN

Cover design by Marylouise E. Doyle.

Cartoons designed by Joe Hoffecker.

Library of Congress Cataloging-in-Publication Data

Frankenberg, Ellen.
    Your family, Inc. : practical tips for building a healthy family business / Ellen Frankenberg.
        p.   cm.
    Includes bibliographical references.
    ISBN 0-7890-0633-2 (hc.: alk. paper).—ISBN 0-7890-0897-1 (pbk.: alk. paper).
    1. Family-owned business enterprises. I. Title.
HD62.25.F73   1999
658'.045—dc21   99-16946
                                                                                                          CIP

CONTENTS

ABOUT THE AUTHOR

Ellen Frankenberg, PhD, is a family psychologist now specializing in consulting to families in business. She has worked intensively with families since 1982, when she launched her practice in the Cincinnati area. A major focus of Dr. Frankenberg's work has been identifying and supporting the growth of healthy families, especially through educational programs that include the whole family. Dr. Frankenberg holds advanced credentials in her field, including a diploma granted by the American Board of Professional Psychology (ABPP) for "advanced competence in the specialty of family psychology." She is a frequent speaker for professional groups such as chambers of commerce, bar associations, chartered life underwriters, etc., as well as the Family Firm Institute, an international organization for consultants to family businesses. In addition, Dr. Frankenberg is a columnist for *Family Business* magazine. Other articles Dr. Frankenberg has written are available at www.familybusinessresources.com.

Foreword

Over 80 percent of the businesses in the United States are family owned and at least partially family operated. Yet until the past two decades little special attention was focused on family businesses, their special intergenerational dynamics, structure and functioning, loyalty bonds and sometimes seething antagonisms, and how to separate the family business from the family's personal life and issues, commonly known today as the business of the family.

Thus, there is a need for materials to help guide members of family business firms and family business families through the labyrinth of complex dilemmas in which many get entangled so that they can maximize their chances of being successful in both realms of their existence. In this compact guidebook, Ellen Frankenberg takes the reader step by step through the typical issues that family businesses confront. For instance, she clearly and succinctly indicates that family members should only be hired for real jobs for which there are real openings and why they should already have the competence required. What will be expected of them, how this will be evaluated, and how they will be compensated should be discussed before they enter the company. She affirms what most family business consultants advocate, that before a member of the next generation joins the family firm, he or she should possess more than the requisite education; in addition, the individual should have acquired on-the-job training of several years in a similar firm and business to gain some experience and prove their mettle.

Frankenberg's style is explicit and easy to follow—whether she is discussing teaching children of wealthy families about the work ethic and the importance of making a contribution, how to manage sibling rivalry in the family firm, the advantages and challenges of preparing one's daughter to become the CEO or CFO, the value of family meetings and family councils, the often thorny problem of choosing a successor, or any number of rather typical concerns. Her approach reflects the wisdom garnered from her experiences, plus a heavy measure of knowledge about family dynamics and functioning, mixed with loads of good common sense.

This handy volume should be a valuable guide and ongoing resource for family business owners, managers, and other members of family business enterprises who want to reflect on their values, beliefs, policies, and procedures, and implement changes necessary to improve their corporate culture and climate as well as their profitability. In addition, it can serve as a refresher course for family business consultants, coaches and mentors, and as a checklist to assist in their assessment and appraisal of and feedback to the families to which they are counseling.

Florence W. Kaslow, PhD
Family Business Consultant
and Family Psychologist
Palm Beach Gardens, Florida

Introduction

Your Family, Inc.: Practical Tips for Building a Healthy Family Business was written for fathers and daughters, mothers and sons, brothers and sisters, grandchildren and uncles and cousins—anyone who shares a family relationship and also a family business.

Blood is thicker than water, they say. Family bonds can endure beyond death and betrayal, beyond bankruptcy and Fortune 500 status. They can also be so complicated that sometimes it feels like you're standing in the middle of a gigantic bowl of emotional spaghetti, with so many connections circling around you that you don't know which end to pick up—and then you get smothered with the sauce of the latest crisis.

This book will focus on a few basic concepts about how healthy families work, how they can work together most effectively in the business they share, and how to sort out the family issues from the business issues. Based on the unique history of your family, this book will help you define and sustain the best of the values that motivated Grandpa long ago, and translate them to the contemporary marketplace, so you can enjoy the next Fourth of July picnic together with more sparklers than ever!

As the prolific World War II generation of entrepreneurs, now in their seventies or eighties, finalize their estate plans, trillions of dollars of value built up in family firms through trillions of too-late nights and too-early mornings will pass to the next generation. Their success or failure as they work through their succession plans affects us all, because 90 percent of U.S. firms are family controlled or operated, including one-third of Fortune 500 companies. They employ 55 percent of the American workforce and produce 49 percent of the gross national product. Less than 15 percent of family businesses survive the third generation.

Although all businesses face intense competition, market shifts, and management failures powerful enough to dismantle them, family businesses face unique challenges, especially concerning transitions from one generation to the next. The founding entrepreneur usually transmits the business to his or her own sons or daughters, raised in the same household, with the same religious values and ethnic traditions, the same work ethic and family expectations, the same holiday recipes and vacations at the beach.

By the third generation, there are seven cousins, born of three marriages, raised in four different households, following one divorce. The natural geometric expansion of the family by the third generation can lead to complex issues such as sibling or cousin rivalry, a more complicated process for choosing a successor among two engineers and three MBAs, and the development of criteria for transmitting stock in a company that probably is "going to be worth something someday."

But families don't have to struggle through these issues alone. Especially since the 1980s, a growing body of research and experience in the elements that build healthy families within healthy family businesses has been developed. This book explores solid information based on family psychology and up-to-date strategies to build a healthy family firm, and at the same time *enrich the relationships* within the family. It offers practical tools to help you capitalize on the powerful emotional currents of energy, commitment, and loyalty that only a family business can provide.

Your Family, Incorporated is designed to be read on a long plane ride. Or it can be used as a stimulus for discussion between spouses, or for gatherings of the whole family at annual meetings. By the end of the book, I hope you will see the patterns and the possibilities—even in the spaghetti—so you can determine which strands to pick up, which to rearrange, which to leave alone, and most important, which to savor.

At the end of life it is said that most people don't say, "I wish I had worked more . . ." Most people seem to savor the relationships, the experiences that offer meaning in life far beyond the workplace. Members of family firms have the opportunity to enjoy both—the pride engendered by building a successful business together, and also the enduring richness of healthy family relationships. I hope this book helps you to savor it all.

Chapter 1

The Geometry of a Healthy Family

One of the best ways to understand the family side of your family business is to dust off your old geometry textbook.

Families begin with the axiom: "The shortest distance between two points is a straight line." The direct, honest communication of young lovers allows little time or energy for third parties to come between them. When they commit themselves to each other and marry, forsaking all others, their challenge is to sustain that direct, honest communication through all the complexity of their lives.

And yet, even while the wedding is being planned, both bride and groom are enmeshed in triangles:

- The triangle between the bride, her mother, and the groom
- The triangle between the groom, his father, and his maxed-out credit card
- The triangle between the brother not chosen as best man, the former girlfriend, the stepmother

Learning to navigate among these triangles and keep communication clean and direct (the shortest distance between two points) is an essential skill for building a healthy family—and a successful family business. Ideally, any two people in a relationship will resolve any differences directly between themselves. Whenever a third party gets in the middle (and hence forms a triangle—see Figure 1.1), the odds of miscommunication increase by 300 percent:

FIGURE 1.1. Miscommunication Triangle

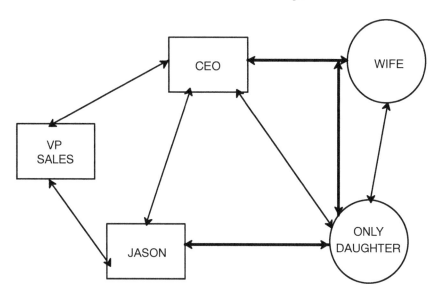

I'll talk to Jim (my VP for Sales) and ask him to go easy on Jason, my new son-in-law, who isn't very thrilled about the machine tool business . . . because my wife will be mad as the devil if he quits and our only daughter moves to Arizona. . . .

Triangles within triangles. Sometimes, even for someone who's used to being a problem solver, the best option is to stay out of the middle of other people's relationships and deal honestly and directly with your own communication—with your son-in-law, your VP, your daughter, and your wife as well.

TIP #1: RECOGNIZE WHEN YOU'RE CAUGHT IN A FAMILY TRIANGLE

Some of the trickiest triangles in a family include ghosts. Sometimes Grandpa's voice is so powerful (even though he was buried in 1978) that it controls today's decisions, blocking action and churning stomachs, even after nine accountants have advised a clear course of action.

"Don't go into debt," Grandpa said. But Grandpa didn't understand the cost of retooling with robotics or developing international markets. Sometimes it helps to clearly recognize which powerful voices from previous generations echo through your head when it's time to make crucial decisions. If you can bring them forward to the front of the stage in your conscious daytime mind, name them, and analyze them in the light of today's data, you can eliminate a triangle with a ghost—a ghost who might have changed his mind had he lived to learn what you now know.

Some family experts say that fundamental attitudes in families—about birth and death, success and failure, risk and security—go back at least seven generations, to your great-grandparents' great-grandparents. These powerful attitudes, transmitted across generations from parent to child by what is said or not said, what is done or not done, are literally *in your bones.* They are as much a part of life as oxygen, and so you assume that these attitudes are "normal": that, for instance, all families will treat sons who don't graduate from medical school as failures, or that all families will celebrate a high school graduation as a crowning achievement. Whether you see yourself today as a success or a failure depends a great deal on your grandfather's dreams.

TIP #2: NAME YOUR FAMILY'S NORMS

Family attitudes or norms, powerful rules transmitted over generations, may have been triggered by some long-forgotten tragedy or triumph, by an emigration or a Great Depression, a great fire, or a great humiliation. You may never know the whole story about the original event that shaped the norm, but if you can put into words the norm you have received from previous generations, bring it to the surface, and examine its value in the

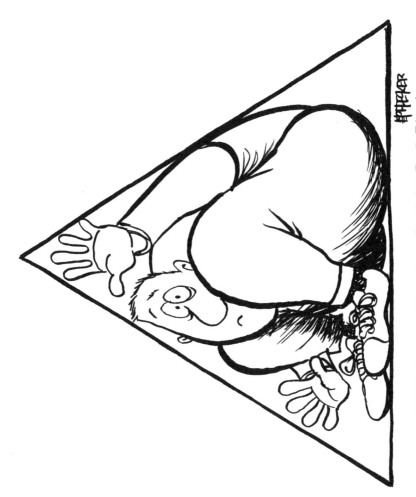

TIP #1. Recognize When You're Caught in a Family Triangle

present, perhaps you can change it. But it is tough work, at least as tough as adapting to the oxygen supply in another altitude, another mountain range.

Family norms are often encapsulated in family sayings: "Keep the Faith," or "Don't move out of the neighborhood," or "Don't tell me bad news," or a personal favorite, "Never say whoa in a horse race or a mud hole." What are the family sayings that you recall? That your children recall?

It's okay to disagree with family sayings or norms, given the data you've collected, the consultants you've paid, and your own informed adult experience. However, if you do disagree with a family norm, you'll probably feel it in your stomach. Over time, like the skier who adapts to high altitudes so he or she can enjoy the most challenging runs again and again, you will get used to it. If you keep functioning within your own best decision-making process, based on your own values and commitments, your stomach will be calmer and Grandpa's voice will be in its own proper place within your memory.

TIP #3: YOU MAY BE A "HERE-AND-NOW" KIND OF GUY, BUT YOUR EMOTIONS MAY BE CAUGHT IN THE PAST

Sometimes triangles keep cropping up in the workplace, based not only on ghosts, but on your own internalized memories of powerful relationships, usually from the nuclear family in which you grew up. Perhaps a gesture, the silhouette of a man of a certain age, a tone of voice, will trigger a memory of the way your father told you to clean out the garage, or the way your eldest sister teased you. And even though you're now forty-two, you may feel, for a moment, as if you're only eight again. When a relationship carries more than the average tension, sometimes it's helpful to sort out when you felt like this before, and how this person is like—or unlike—the powerful family voices that shaped you long ago.

Once you can identify which powerful person from your own past (the idealized father who died when you were fourteen? the mother who abandoned you? the grandmother who criticized every haircut you ever got?) reminds you the most of the "difficult" person among your current difficult relationships, you can step out of the triangle and get back to choosing the shortest distance between two points: clear, direct communication based on the observable facts and circumstances in front of you here and now.

How is this person *different* from your father, your grandmother, or whomever's memory he or she kindles? If you can't immediately name any differences, that's a big clue that this person has psychologically stepped right into the shoes of some powerful person in your past, even though he or she may be of a different gender, generation, educational level, occupation, family background, physique, ethnic tradition, political persuasion, religious identity, and so on.

TIP #4: SOMETIMES EVERYDAY RELATIONSHIPS BECOME FAMILIAR

Perhaps for some ancient evolutionary reason, we continue to be attracted to what is "familiar" in the original sense of that word. No matter what kind of organization you're working with, you may confer family emotional power on team members who aren't genetic family, and calibrate your responses to them on the basis of outdated family dynamics.

Our minds work this way because one of the cardinal rules of psychology is that *perception is selective.* Two witnesses of the same traffic accident will recall different details. Two persons meeting the same new individual will also recall different aspects of that person's appearance or behavior. We pay attention to what attracts our interest, usually similarities called up from forgotten files in our memories. Our minds, like heat-seeking missiles, hone in on our own personal links with powerful past relationships, whenever they pop up in the locker room, the copier room, or the boardroom.

The differences between this current person who gives you difficulty and your internalized memory of some family member *are inevitably greater than the similarities*. It takes deliberate, concentrated effort to discover the differences, and then to relate to this person, this co-worker, here and now, by focusing on his or her uniqueness, the differences rather than the similarities. She only happens to have a voice that sounds just like Grandma's.

TIP #5: IN A FAMILY FIRM, YOUR FATHER'S VOICE MAY REALLY BE THE CEO'S VOICE

In a family business, the man who continues to direct your work may, in fact, be your father. Because family business members often stay in day-to-day contact with parents much longer than their peers, it's important to understand not only triangles, but also circles, or the perimeters around relationships. It's important to be able to draw a circle around yourself, defining how you are a unique individual, even as you stand in the middle of five brothers who look a great deal like you.

Defining who you are as an individual *adult* is also crucial to working together within a family business in which day-to-day parent-child relationships may be lifelong. One of the best ways to do this is to have some real-world experience of autonomy, ideally before joining the business. Earning a college degree remains an important ticket for entrance to adulthood and management jobs in most U.S. companies, and a family member should earn some kind of valid ticket to quality as a hire.

Many family firms require that the next generation meet at least the same standards as other hires for the same responsibilities, including passing the same drug screen! Some family firms require their own members to operate within the family's defined ethical standards, and to *exceed* the standards for other hires. If standards for hiring family members are clear, when Dad's voice hits your pager one more time, you will know that he speaks to you as a co-worker who's getting the job done, and not as a child who's late for dinner again.

TIP #6: QUALIFY YOURSELF, SO YOU STAND ON YOUR OWN CREDENTIALS

If you're not into rural sociology or the advanced algebra courses required for a bachelor's degree, check out a two-year degree in a technical college, or an apprenticeship that meets the standards of your company's trade—as an electrician, a stone cutter, or a pastry chef. Qualify yourself, so there can be no question in your mind, or anyone else's, that you can stand on your own credentials, and meet the requirements for the job published in the newspaper ad for all comers.

> Two sons of a founding entrepreneur, who had descended from a long line of German bakers, graduated from a topflight college prep high school in Ohio. Instead of heading off to college, they decided to enroll in a rigorous three-year internship program for pastry chefs in Germany, so they could continue the tradition of fine bakery goods in their family firm. Their sister became the first graduate in an entrepreneurship program in the business school of a local university.

TIP #7: IF YOU PLAN TO WORK IN THE FAMILY FIRM, GET OUT OF TOWN

Even if Dad is offering you a new sales territory, a 50K salary plus expenses, and a new Pontiac Grand Am (for business use, of course) starting July 1, get out of town. Get a job with a sister company one step ahead of your own, preferably in another market area, and stay long enough to get at least one promotion, usually two or three years. You will then know for the rest of your life—and every employee in "Dad's company" will know—that you can make it on your own, and that you have something to offer to take the family firm to the next level of development.

Another way to develop individual autonomy, especially during times of exploding international trade, is to get an internship in Slovakia or Singapore, with the opportunity to learn another language and how to do business in a culture where all the rules are different. A tour of duty in the Air Force or the Navy can also offer a prospective heir, especially in peacetime, the chance to learn not only technical skills, but how to start from the bottom of a very different kind of organization in which your family name has less to do with your first promotion than your survival skills in boot camp.

And even if you have worked from high school on in "the shop," and never moved out of town, hopefully you have developed some way to become your own person outside the family, by heading up a volunteer organization, remodeling your first home, sailing solo across Lake Michigan, or skiing in mountain ranges where no one else in your family has ever gone.

As a result, you can draw a clear circle around your own accomplishments—what belongs to you as an individual—in contrast to what you have inherited from your family, or what belongs to the family firm.

TIP #8: WHEN YOU'RE IN THE FAMILY CIRCLE, RESPECT ITS BOUNDARIES

It's also important to be able to draw clear circles, with your dusty compass, not only around your own experience, but also around the perimeters of your relationship between yourself and your spouse, around you and your nuclear family, and around you and your extended family. Last night's squabble between Mom and Dad won't become gossip on the shop floor, because you and your brothers and sisters, or you and your sons and daughters, clearly understand that family squabbles—and their resolution—belong within the family, and outside the business circle.

Understanding these boundaries can help individuals know where they stand in the family, and can actually increase intimacy within family relationships (where it belongs) because each one knows that secrets and vulnerabilities will be protected. "Good fences make good neighbors," said Robert Frost, a wise American poet. In more practical terms for those at work in family firms, good boundaries make good relationships within families.

TIP #9: KEEP YOUR BUSINESS OUT OF THE FAMILY PARTY

Understanding circles in a family business also means that you can draw a line around the business, and leave it out of the birthday party. It means that family members not employed in the business can look forward to Thanksgiving dinner, without dreading relentless talk about new marketing schemes and old marketing triumphs. It also means that there are very good reasons why family members who don't work for the company are not included in business meetings, but have other appropriate ways to express their concerns about the business (see Figure 1.2).

As a family member, I need to know when I'm inside the family circle, gathered around the Thanksgiving table, which is round. The person who sits at the "head" of the table may vary from year to year, depending on who's hosting the holiday dinner. The eldest and the youngest adult siblings can now gather there as equals, each responsible for his or her own life, but sharing a profound bond, an emotional history built from bad

FIGURE 1.2. Family Circle

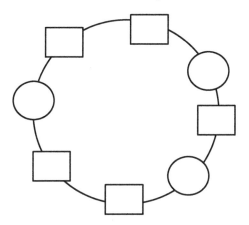

jokes and silly tears, pillow fights and pumpkins, and failed as well as triumphant recipes for the stuffing in the turkey.

TIP #10: CONSENSUS, CONSENSUS, CONSENSUS

The experience of the family circle leads family firm members to prefer consensus as a way of making decisions, as documented by the 1995 Massachusetts Mutual Life Insurance Company survey of family business owners.[1] The myth of the patriarch dominating all decision making doesn't hold up for the majority of family firms: families want to be able to celebrate Thanksgiving together, and so they will struggle longer, compared to other organizations, to try to reach consensus and build support for major decisions *before* they disrupt that powerful family circle.

At their worst, because they lack the skills to reach consensus, family firms can be frosted into indecision, because some choices may upset family members, and the leadership may not want to take a tough stand—not only because of Grandpa's ghost but because of their very much alive brothers and sisters, who sit across the table from them today, and will be there tomorrow too.

One tough decision affecting many family businesses is the choice of a successor. Only one of the seven cousins in the third generation will be named CEO. Only one name can be signed as CHIEF Executive Officer, and only one signature is required for many lucrative contracts. Building consensus on tough issues such as choosing a leader from the next generation is not a quick project. It requires the family to build skills and understanding—not only about the business, but also about each other and the history and values that shape the unique decision-making style for this family at this time in its history and in its future.

TIP #11: YOUR COMPANY WILL TURN OUT TO BE A TRIANGLE

Once the family reaches consensus, and selects its most competent leader, the structure of the business becomes—surprise!—a triangle. Even though there may be teams working on specific projects, in the end, in corporate America, all reporting systems lead to the top of the pyramid where, the inimitable Harry Truman said, "The buck stops here."

Working within the pyramidal structure of the corporation means that you know your job within the hierarchy, and contribute from your position to the overall growth of the company. It means that promotions are based on competency, and on the skills and aptitudes required by the firm at this point in its evolution. It also means that if your younger brother has the right tickets to be president, and you're better at outside sales, so be it. You're still the quarterback when you play touch football on Thanksgiving Day.

Chapter 2

Know Which Hat You Are Wearing:
The Business Hat or the Family Hat

Far beyond the 8-to-5 schedule of most workers, the entrepreneurs I know are focused on their businesses, even when they are on the golf course or the plane ride back from Dallas. Their best inspirations often *do* come in the shower, or on the seventeenth fairway. "If your name's on the door, you care a lot more" is the slogan of a Cincinnati hardware chain, and it's true, especially in times of turmoil or transition. Business thinking can absorb every waking moment.

But in managing a *family* business, sometimes a *family* crisis can upset your concentration, even on the seventeenth fairway or in the midst of a major meeting:

> Your daughter Rachel calls to announce that she really does want a job in the company after she graduates from Iowa State in June. You know that she barely passed her domestic science courses, and your son has told you he will quit if his little sister, the ditsy one, ever sets foot in the plant.

TIP #12: RECOGNIZE WHEN YOU'RE BEING ASKED
TO RESPOND AS A FAMILY MEMBER
AND WHEN YOU'RE NOT

When the phone call is from a family member, hold the phone until you put on your family hat. Then respond to your lovely

Know Which Hat You Are Wearing: The Business Hat or the Family Hat

daughter as a concerned parent would, affirming her desire to get a great job. But you can also explain that you can't make a business decision at that moment, *because you're not wearing your business hat!* But you'll be glad to tell her about the current openings in the company, and help her decide whether she meets the criteria for any particular job.

When you're wearing your family hat, you recognize that you're speaking what is almost a unique, private language, with different rules and expectations, based on values, or patterns of belief, which have been built up over generations, as countless daughters have asked their fathers for favors, and their fathers have responded with as much courage as they could summon.

Although each family is unique, and no one—especially outsiders—can predict how a particular family will react, there are also many ways in which families are similar. The following four characteristics describe the ways many families in business together operate:

1. Families prefer *privacy.* They really don't want anybody to know their net worth, or the stories about Uncle Will who stayed until the last call at every bar in Syracuse, and regularly drained Grandma's bank account. A healthy sense of privacy within a family can also create the possibility that if you do share a problem, your secret will be kept.
2. Families are built through *emotional bonds*, forged over generations of mealtimes and bedtimes, tears and triumphs. Those you love the most can make you the most angry, and the most proud, and be the most difficult to fire. Blood is thicker than water.
3. Families, ideally, are grounded in *acceptance,* so you can still come home again, even if you miss the shot at the buzzer in the state basketball tournament, or get indicted for income tax evasion.

4. Families cherish *tradition*. They really do want to have Mom's double chocolate cake for the birthday dinner, and the annual softball game on the Fourth of July. Even though politics and economics and even religions may change, there are some traditions in families that wise men and women don't mess with.

And so, when you're operating within the family circle, wearing your family hat, you are probably strongly influenced by family characteristics such as these, reinforced generation after generation.

TIP #13: KNOW WHAT'S INSIDE YOUR FAMILY CIRCLE

Privacy
Emotional Bonds
Acceptance
Tradition

Of course, the ways these norms are expressed in different families vary enormously. Some families consider talk about sex to fall clearly within the norm of privacy, so much so that it is *never* discussed. Other families talk about it as a normal part of life, in a relaxed, comfortable way:

One family I know had developed a set of signals about respecting privacy for lovemaking: when the shades were drawn in the bedroom window at Grandma and Grandpa's house, everyone knew it was not a good time to ring the doorbell. A different family would probably never acknowledge that Grandma and Grandpa knew anything at all about such afternoon delights.

The best way to find out about these private understandings within a family other than the one in which you were raised is by marrying into it. But even then, no one will explain all this in advance, because they all believe there's no other way to function, and you will probably have to discover the private rules by breaking them. At the rehearsal dinner before the wedding, if you try to hug everyone in a family that doesn't believe in hugging, don't be surprised if they back off stiffly, leaving you puzzled and feeling awkward, even though no one said a critical word.

What generates emotion also varies greatly between families, which you learned if you ever tried to tell a joke about Democrats in a family that regularly votes for Democrats. Nor can you assume that the death of a family member will universally cause sadness. Sometimes a death after long suffering brings tremendous relief; sometimes the deceased had demeaned so many family members for so many years that no one sheds an honest tear at the funeral.

Acceptance in a healthy family extends across genders and generations, across foibles and failures. A family that accepts all children equally will offer their daughters the same options to develop their talents as their sons, and Charlie, who has attention deficit disorder and can't sit through an American history class, will be encouraged to find his unique path, even if it's not through the doors of Dad's alma mater.

Acceptance does not mean denying abuse, or putting up with addictions to alcohol or drugs, without attempting to intervene. Precisely because the family values its own inner, private circle and its unique emotional bonds, acceptance means that you can come home again *if* you resolve your legal problems, or get sober, or quit insulting other family members, or accept professional help when problems persist without it.

Tradition sustains the branches of the family tree, when strong winds and hailstorms buffet them. It provides predictability and a sense of belonging. We know what the dressing in the turkey is supposed to taste like, even if your prospective daughter-in-law politely compliments you for your failed effort.

But tradition can also be a burden if it becomes rigid, for example, if only the eldest son is groomed to become CEO because the eldest sons in previous generations always rose to the occasion.

> Another tradition that had outlived its usefulness was practiced by a family-owned brewery, which gave every worker a case of cold beer each Friday afternoon, as part of their wages. This tradition was sadly but wisely deleted after one too many DUIs, and increasing awareness of a rising population of alcoholics on the payroll.

Sometimes, in the light of present knowledge, tough decisions have to be made that alter traditional expectations, even though we feel the criticism, or the gravel churning in the gut. The unique convolutions in our brains, our neural pathways, are shaped by hundreds of repetitions of the same exercises of thought. It's hard to reshape convolutions etched by habit and expectation, but sometimes the business requires it:

> Your Chief Operating Officer tells you that the company's market share has dropped dramatically during the past twelve months, and proposes that you develop a new initiative for international marketing, which will effectively wipe out family members' distributions this year. You know by heart the complaints you will hear, and which family members will voice them.

TIP #14: KNOW WHAT'S INSIDE
YOUR BUSINESS CIRCLE

When you take off your family hat and focus intently on the business, an entirely different set of expectations shapes your thinking and your behavior, whether you are aware of it or not. Your decisions are informed by another set of realities:

1. Your business has accountability beyond the family, to its employees, its customers, its suppliers, its creditors, its community. It has a *public* identity, which means it has taxes to pay, OSHA requirements to meet, advertising to shape, and a reputation for quality and reliability to sustain.
2. Businesses rise and fall on the basis of numbers: productivity, sales, inventory, market share, profitability. The analysis of *data* forms the basis for sharp decision making, even though this can at times force the entrepreneur to make tough choices.
3. The selection and promotion of personnel in a successful business is based on *competence.* Developing criteria for hiring based on the requirements of the company, and promoting candidates with the best fit for the company's goals within the special demands of its industry, are part of the professionalization of a family firm.
4. Successful companies are adaptive, constantly *changing* to meet the needs of the marketplace and the competition. The strategic business plan is out of date every eighteen months, because that's about how long it takes for a new wave of technology to hit the beaches.

And so, when you're wearing your business hat, focusing on the tough choices, you're deep inside a different circle:

Business Circle

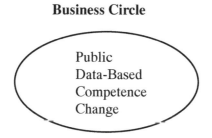

Public
Data-Based
Competence
Change

Businesses that operate like private country clubs for the benefit of family members alone make the adage "Rags to riches to rags in three generations" come true all over again. Every business has a public trust because its products and services, its bankers, its employees and customers require that the company manage its resources in a businesslike manner.

If Dad wants to use the credit line to buy a top-of-the-line corporate jet in a year when no one gets a raise, will anyone challenge him? Do you really believe that family members who work for the company are accountable? Or can they manipulate funds behind the scenes in questionable ways, to provide perks for family members who can "bleed" the company others have worked so hard to build? The family's norm of privacy probably won't cover all these sins. Sooner or later, the truth will come out.

TIP #15: DEVELOP STRATEGIES TO KEEP THE FAMILY FIRM ACCOUNTABLE

Developing a competent group of advisors, including the corporate attorney or accountant, or CEOs in noncompeting industries, can provide balance for a family entrepreneur. These advisors, meeting quarterly, can provide a sounding board for new strategies, or alert the CEO *before* the company starts to bleed red ink. Such a group of hand-picked, trusted consultants is especially important in a family firm, because they can keep the CEO honest about family compensation, and also counterbalance the emotional power of the family, when it's time to make tough business decisions.

Sometimes the CEO can benefit from joining a group of peers who were not raised in the same family. The YPO (Young Presidents Organization) or TEC (The Executive Committee) or a support group of noncompetitive CEOs organized through a local chamber of commerce can provide confidential advice and education about solid business practices.

Some firms have found that open-book management systems motivate employees, because they learn to connect their own productivity with clear financial benefits. Perhaps family members can also be educated about the real implications of the balance sheet through regular reports about the hard numbers, before distributions are increased—or cut.

TIP #16: BUSINESS DECISIONS NEED TO BE MADE FOR BUSINESS REASONS

Sayings such as, "He who dies with the most data wins!" affect family firms as they plunge headlong into the information age. As more sophisticated information systems become available to small firms, balancing them against the megacorporations, family firms will be compelled to make more decisions on the basis of data, rather than emotional pressure from the family alone.

Some families will always offer jobs to members who have limitations; hopefully even those jobs will be based on the actual needs of the company, justified through the numbers, and defined by the competencies of the family member—whether it's supervising a warehouse, or answering the phone from a wheelchair. Creating jobs for family members who really can't perform a specific function is demeaning to them, enables them to maintain dependence, and builds resentment in the workforce. Caring for relatives in need belongs, first of all, within the generosity of the family circle, unless management can find creative ways to effectively harness their unique talents for the good of the business.

You discover that your youngest son, who barely got a GED because of a "learning disability," has become a computer

whiz and a very valuable asset for the family firm. The
$10,000 you skeptically agreed to pay him, as an indepen-
dent contractor, to build and manage a Web site for the
family firm has turned into nearly $500,000 in new sales in
its first year of operation.

The selection of competent leadership, especially when heading into the second and third generations, is the fork in the road
that sometimes leads in surprising directions, or can destroy
some venerable family firms. Businesses that hire or promote,
not on the basis of competence, but simply because of blood or
marriage, are doomed to fail, probably not with a bang, but a
whimper.

Perhaps your new son-in-law, the outdoor guy with the fresh
associate's degree in landscape architecture, really will fit into
the machine tool shop, and your only daughter won't move with
him to Arizona. But if you have on your business hat, before
offering him the job, you have to ask yourself, "Does he really
have the basic competencies to join the company at the management level? Would I hire him if Jennifer hadn't fallen in love
with him? Will my relationship with Jennifer and her new family
be better if it's not complicated by business issues?"

Even if, according to the family tradition, all new in-laws
expect to be offered jobs and all family members (regardless of
their drug habits) have been kept on the payroll, when you put on
your business hat, you may change this custom, because it is not
in the best interest of the company.

And even if family members who do not work in the company
have become accustomed to annual $100,000 distributions, and
the company needs to retool, perhaps distributions to family
members will be cut this year, because it is not in the best interest
of the company.

If your grandfather's dreams do come true, and your company
triples in size, there will be even more changes for family mem-

bers to absorb. That old folksy, kitchen feeling, with family members dropping in and out of the office offering free advice and criticism, will be gone. The culture of a company with $100 million annual sales is dramatically different than a mom-and-pop start-up, and the family may have to adapt to the new way of doing business. In the long run, their trust funds will be richer, but some of the changes will feel uncomfortable because the roles of family members and the roles of business employees will be more clearly defined.

TIP #17: THE PRIORITIES OF THE FAMILY AND THE PRIORITIES OF THE BUSINESS ARE OPPOSITES

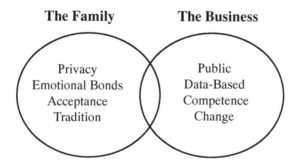

The Family

Privacy
Emotional Bonds
Acceptance
Tradition

The Business

Public
Data-Based
Competence
Change

The most important key to working through the dilemmas that face families in business together is knowing what role you're playing at which time. When are you standing in the business circle, dealing with public accountability, data-based decisions, hiring the most competent candidates, and constantly forecasting change? When do you need to be standing within the family circle, sustaining its privacy, its emotional bonds, its acceptance of each member, and its preference for its best traditions? When are you caught in the vortex between them?

Chapter 3

Ownership Has Its Privileges,
and Its Hazards . . .

A third hat hangs on the hat rack in the hallway in your family firm: the hat you wear as an owner. Even though you already wear one hat as a family member valuing privacy, emotional bonds, acceptance, and tradition, and another as a business executive, valuing your public identity, data analysis, competence, and capacity for change, there is another broad-brimmed hat you wear for other special occasions:

> After turning over the job of CEO to your thirty-six-year-old son so you can work harder on your golf game, you show up for the annual stockholders meeting to find that expenses are up 17 percent (new furnishings for the executive office suite and an executive "team-building" adventure in Cancun) and profits are flat . . .

Family business owners, especially the retired variety, have a unique set of priorities, and they enjoy taking pride in the company's accomplishments. Even if they spend every winter in Sarasota, they still hold informal power, ready to pick up the phone or breeze into the office on a moment's notice:

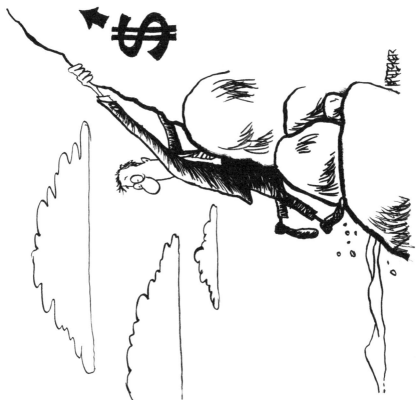

Ownership Has Its Privileges, and Its Hazards . . . .

1. Having mortgaged their starter home to the rafters, and eaten lots of macaroni and cheese suppers in their twenties and thirties, founding entrepreneurs want to make a profit.
2. Most business owners don't like surprises. They want timely *information,* before the bankers and the creditors get it, so they can make well-informed decisions, including when to change the next generation's stock allocation or fire the CEO.
3. The owners I know are fascinated by good *management.* After they retire, they will spend hours talking with their fellow entrepreneurs about their own "war stories"—what worked and what didn't—and who is not to be trusted, even if it's one's own son-in-law.
4. Whether they are former employees, or inherited stock and never worked within the company, or are part of the management team, owners want *marketability;* they want to know that their products or services are doing well in the marketplace, and that the company itself is marketable, in the event that the family decides to sell it.

This means that those who hold stock in the family firm focus on the goals within yet another circle, the circle of ownership:

Ownership

Profit
Information
Management
Marketability

So now participants in a family business can clearly see the three-ring circus in which they stand, inside and between the three circles of ownership, family membership and business leadership. Renate Tagiuri and John Davis first introduced these circles to describe the experience within the family firm; their work provides a helpful basis for our deepening understanding of family business dynamics.[1]

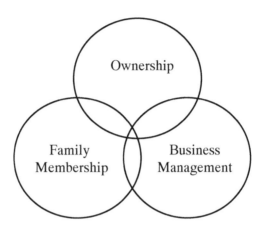

TIP #18: OWNERSHIP IN A FAMILY FIRM
IS A JOB TOO; DOING IT RIGHT
CAN MEAN THE DIFFERENCE
BETWEEN DISASTER AND SUCCESS

Owners of successful family firms may sometimes find themselves standing in the wedge—the vortex between the requirements of the business, the emotional bonds of the family, and the fiduciary obligations of ownership. Knowing where you stand is always a first step in clarifying where to go next.

Owners of family firms also recognize that their whole enterprise stands within other circles too. They recognize, upon reflection, that they hold the company in trust not only because of their own dividend checks, or their family's benefit, but also because their decisions affect employees, customers, suppliers, and the communities in which the company is located (see Figure 3.1).

FIGURE 3.1. Circles

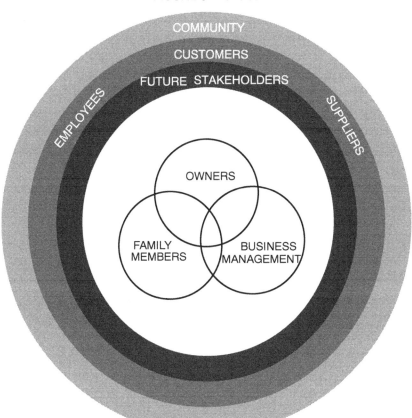

Owners' decisions affect not only those sitting around the table at the annual meeting this year, but also the family's children yet unborn, and all the future stakeholders who stand to inherit or not inherit the wealth and heritage of the family firm.

Seven cousins, all in their sixties, owners of inherited stock in a fourth-generation lumber company, gather in their attorney's offices to discuss whether to initiate a lawsuit challenging the eighth cousin, the present CEO. There have been no distributions for the past five years, nor has there been any agreement on the value of the nonvoting shares they hold, if they wish to redeem them. They have reason to believe that the company is highly profitable, and have been advised that, since other attempts have failed, their only remaining option, to get complete disclosure and a fair buy-out, is litigation. Going to court is distasteful to all of them, since they have always considered themselves a warm, close-knit family, and continue to celebrate the holidays together. But they want to finalize their own estate plans, and spare their descendents continuing acrimony . . .

Owners sometimes inherit stock without any choice and, particularly if they hold a minority position in a large, multigeneration family, may have little control over decisions by the company's management. Their options have been: keep quiet to avoid conflict; moral persuasion; sell their stock back to the company, within the limited market of a minority shareholder; maintain confidence that ultimately the integrity of the firm's leadership will prevail; and, if all else fails, litigation—a tragedy in any family.

Family firm owners can focus on strategies to prevent a crisis that is volatile enough to disrupt family relationships. Some of these strategies need to be implemented by the ownership long before a potential crisis erupts.

One of the chief tasks for those who own stock in a family firm is to engender respect for ownership within the next generation. Children can resent the company that demands so much time and hard work of parents; or they may feel pressure to work there, even when their talents lie in the ballet rather than in the bottling industry. Sometimes parents share very little about the scope and significance of the firm with their children, attempting to shield them from feeling entitled to too many privileges, too much wealth.

What ownership means differs widely between families: sometimes it means cashing a generous check at the end of each fiscal year; sometimes ownership means pitching in during busy seasons, or during a crisis such as a fire or flood; sometimes it means lending expertise to the company on particular projects, such as developing an employee handbook or writing the minutes of family meetings. And sometimes ownership is a headache, with little perceivable benefit to the individual stockholder. Some would rather have their inheritance invested in other, more liquid investments.

The healthiest business families I know take ownership seriously, and transmit stock only to those family members who have the maturity and capability to continually educate themselves about the company and its industry, so they can make informed decisions when the company reaches a turning point.

TIP #19: BEFORE TRANSMITTING STOCK, THINK IT OVER TWICE: WOULD I WANT THIS RELATIVE MAKING DECISIONS ABOUT MY FUTURE LIVELIHOOD?

The Native Americans of the past understood very clearly what it means to hold an asset in trust, whether that asset was the Black Hills of South Dakota, the salmon streams of the Pacific Northwest, or the herds of buffalo on the Great Plains. They made decisions on the basis of how their choices would affect their descendants seven generations after them. Instead of ownership as we define it today in legal terms, they considered themselves "stewards," taking care of the resources around them during their lifetimes, so future generations could enjoy a similar bounty.

Although owners of family firms vary greatly from the ancient tribes of North America, they do share with them a preference for the long view, for planning that often extends into the next generation, in sharp contrast to other U.S. corporations which focus so intently on the next market cycle. Family firms are precisely designed to think about consequences of present decisions on future generations. At their best, they are designed to make decisions, not from an individualistic perspective, but on the basis of what will benefit the whole, the tribe, the kinship, the family.

TIP #20: OWNERSHIP IN A FAMILY FIRM MEANS LEARNING HOW TO BUILD CONSENSUS, CONSENSUS, CONSENSUS

Very often, busy entrepreneurs and their families have had little opportunity to learn the skills to build the consensus within the family that they will need when an enticing offer to sell is on the table, or when the CEO dies in the night with no heir apparent.

Although one often hears the statistic that fewer than 15 percent of family firms in the United States survive the third generation, those strong companies that do survive may have particular characteristics in common with some of the long-lived companies of Europe, where it is not uncommon to find firms passing from seventh- or ninth-generation owners.

Barbara Wall, writing in the *International Herald Tribune* in 1997 described Les Henokians, an organization for long-lived family firms in Europe.[2] These family firms:

- possessed a clear sense of at least 200 years of family history;
- selected competent nonfamily managers when needed;
- excluded incompetent family members from management;
- developed ways to sustain family control, especially through self-financing; and
- stuck close to their basic product range.

This means that they reached a common understanding about the significance of their own history, and that they had developed consistent policies, especially regarding the selection of managers and the role of the family in relationship to the business. They had developed the skills to build consensus among family members about significant issues that impacted the continuity of their firms.

TIP #21: AS AN OWNER, TAKE THE LONG VIEW

As an owner who takes the long view and supports the building of consensus as the preferred means to sustain family decision making, here are some tough questions to consider:

1. *Do you want to transmit company shares to each of your descendents equally, for example, 25 percent to each of your four children, whether they work in the company or not?* This means that within two or three generations, ownership will be scattered across the country and across the psyches of your unknown great-grandchildren. How will that affect the family's capability to build informed consensus? If you choose to do this, what strategies will need to be implemented so that future owners are prepared to exercise their privileges appropriately?

2. *Do you want to focus ownership among those who work in the company, and distribute other assets to your children who choose not to work in the company?* Often real estate or life insurance are used to provide comparable—if not equal—assets to siblings who choose another path. However, once the value of the company exceeds $10 million, how much life insurance or real estate can you provide? The reality remains that the family firm may be the most significant asset the family will ever possess, and other assets may never turn out to be equal. What is ultimately fair is not always equal.

3. *Do you want to develop two classes of stock—voting and nonvoting?* This strategy is often suggested by legal advis-

ors as a way of sharing wealth within the family, while retaining control among those close to the company's operations. But what is the value of nonvoting stock, if future management reduces dividends and provides no forum for clear information about the company's prospects? What is the value of nonvoting stock if future management is chosen from outside the family, and there is no structure in place to provide good information and sustain family control?

4. *Do you really want to transmit stock in a manner based primarily on strategies to avoid estate taxes?* Many parents take advantage of the option to gift $10,000 in stock value each year to their children or grandchildren, as a means to reduce their own tax obligations. But how then will they prepare the younger generation for the implications of ownership? Is each grandchild capable of accepting that responsibility? How will such a dispersal of stock affect the future management of the company, especially those family members who do make the commitment to work for the company and may end up in a minority position?

TIP #22: THE KEY TO HEALTHY OWNERSHIP OF THE FAMILY FIRM IS THE SAME AS THE KEY TO ANY SIGNIFICANT INVESTMENT: INFORMATION, INFORMATION, INFORMATION

Wall Street has danced around "insider information" for decades. Family firms are full of the ultimate insiders. They hear rumors long before they hit the street, and they often sleep with the decision makers. And yet some widows still have no idea of the value of the company until the attorney reads the will. According to a 1997 Arthur Andersen survey of family firms, one-fourth of shareholders have no knowledge of the senior generation's stock transfer plans.[3]

Healthy ownership of family firms means developing legitimate systems to share solid, timely information, so family members don't have to gossip, or manipulate other family members, or litigate to get the reports that stockholders in other corporations can get with a phone call.

Some families have developed an organized structure, such as a family forum, which allows all the stakeholders in the family—those who stand to gain or lose, depending on the success or failure of the company—to come together in a supportive environment, to learn about the company. The whole family can then contribute their own ideas and concerns, especially regarding company policies that affect family participation in the firm. This structure, used wisely, is the single most effective tool owners can use to prevent future family conflict. It provides family owners with an opportunity to assess the current performance of the company and its management, and to raise questions directly, before a rumor mill of misinformation is organized (see Figure 3.2).

TIP #23: IF YOU BUILD A FAMILY FORUM, THEY WILL COME

The family forum provides an opportunity for all family members—usually sixteen years of age and older—to recognize their own family history and values as a basis for decision making. It can provide practical opportunities for learning how to communicate across generations, how to resolve conflict, how to build consensus before a buyout offer hits the table, or how to choose a successor. It also provides a healthy opportunity for the younger generation to develop pride in the company, especially before they choose their own careers.

The family forum also ensures that business decisions will be made in their proper context, by the executive team in consultation with other business advisors. How to organize a family forum will be discussed in more detail in Chapter 7.

Besides making a profit and protecting that profit through timely information, owners also have the obligation to select

FIGURE 3.2. Family Forum

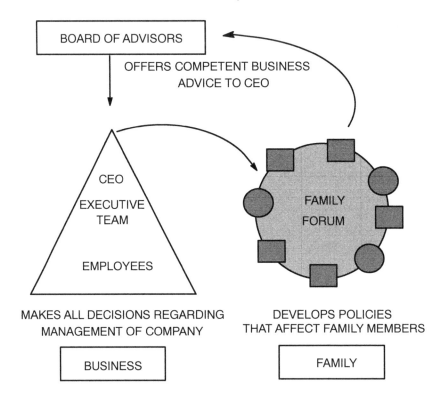

good management—the key to the future success of any company. In the first generation the owner and the management are usually synonymous, but in later generations the owner or owners will need to select management from among several candidates within the family, or from a pool of qualified nonfamily candidates.

Some owners may spend more time developing a game plan for their son's Saturday afternoon soccer game than they do developing a succession plan for the family firm. Developing a plan that ensures good management for the next generation in the family firm is perhaps the toughest task business owners face, and most owners get to do it only once.

Succession planning involves dealing with death, and the recognition that even the founding entrepreneur is not indispensable. It includes assessing not only the requirements of the business, which can often be done quantitatively, but also assessing the capabilities of individual family members—a qualitative task that touches much deeper chords in the human emotional repertoire:

> A family with four sons, all in their thirties, and each intelligent, competent, and committed to working in the company, begins to face the task of naming the next CEO. Their father, the very effective founder of a profitable, expanding company, believes that he should not retire until one of his sons has been named to head the company. He wants to select the best candidate, given the future needs of the company and its industry. He does not necessarily believe that the eldest should automatically be appointed, especially because his sons are quite close in age and represent different capabilities.

TIP #24: DEVELOP CRITERIA FOR FUTURE LEADERSHIP IN ADVANCE

One option to make the choice for future leadership—perhaps the single most significant decision to put the company in the 15 percent that survive the crucial third generation—is to develop criteria for the company's future leadership in advance. Then all comers—and their spouses and in-laws—know what is expected. The criteria need to recognize the needs of the company and the direction its industry is taking, as well as the history and values of this unique family. These criteria can be discussed in a family forum, so that qualified candidates can be prepared, and the family can eventually support the choice of successor.

Here are some initial questions owners may want to ask themselves in order to tailor the criteria for the next CEO to the specific needs of the company, *before* the present CEO gets hit by a truck:

1. What *technical* skills are required to lead this company? (If this is a computer software firm, does the CEO need technical proficiency?)
2. What *management* skills are required to lead this company? (Will an MBA be an advantage to the leader of this company five years from now? Ten years from now?)
3. What hands-on business *experience* is required to lead this company? (Has the candidate worked for another company successfully? Or headed up a department or division of this company successfully?)
4. What *people skills* are required to lead this company? (Can the candidate communicate effectively with a range of constituents: bankers, union leaders, other CEOs, family members, employees?)
5. Given the *direction of the industry*, what particular skills are required? (Is this industry facing consolidation, so that negotiating experience, sophisticated financial knowledge, or strategic planning skills are essential assets?)
6. What kind of *vision for the future* is needed by this company now? (Is the candidate capable of managing the $50 million company this firm can become within ten years? What is his or her vision for the future? Is his or her vision compatible with the family's vision?)

Owners of a family firm may consider questions such as these and reach the conclusion that there is no family member who meets the requirements for leading this family firm at this point in time. Their fiduciary responsibility may call them to appoint a nonfamily executive, even though their emotions, their dreams, would lead them to appoint their only son, whom they dearly love, but who loves snowboarding in Colorado more.

If the family owners select the best possible management for the company at this time in its development, and continue to maintain judicious control, the odds increase that the company will be successful enough to appoint another family member as CEO in the future, perhaps a grandson yet unborn.

Two titans of American commerce, the Ford Motor Co. and Motorola, recently appointed grandsons of previous leaders to executive positions, after interim professional management. Smaller family firms can retain that option, especially if they utilize a structure such as a family forum to continually define the values and the mission of the family.

In addition to profit, timely information, and good management, owners value marketability. They want to know that their products or services have value in the marketplace, and that the firm itself is worth a good price. They don't want to be producing buggy whips in cyberspace. This means that each generation must, in fact, reinvent the company, especially since most products enjoy approximately a twenty-three-year market cycle, according to the research of Ernesto Pozo.[4]

TIP #25: EACH GENERATION MUST REINVENT THE COMPANY THROUGH INNOVATION, INNOVATION, INNOVATION

Effective owners must be prepared to support innovation from the next generation, at least to regenerate their own investment, their own retirement income. You can't run your grandfather's company anymore, and you probably can't run your father's company either. Even if you produce a perennial product such as Tootsie Rolls or Smuckers' jams, which continue to enjoy good market share, marketing strategies or production techniques will continually evolve in directions Grandpa couldn't imagine.

And so, when you are wearing your owner's hat, with your focus on profit, timely information, good management, and marketability, you provide an important balance to those whose primary focus is either on the family or on the day-to-day operations of the business. You provide the long view, the fiduciary responsibility that looks beyond the immediate crisis to future potential, even when choices are difficult. And you enjoy the benefits of a very rich heritage, built from your own sweat equity, and the struggles of those upon whose shoulders you stand.

Chapter 4

Competition in the Family Firm: Sibling Rivalry

Sibling rivalry began with the book of Genesis, the story of the oldest human family of all. Cain, the eldest brother, became a farmer, and brought his first fruits to Yahweh as a gift. But Yahweh favored the gift of Abel, the younger son, the shepherd, over Cain's gifts, leading to great jealousy on Cain's part. Fratricide shattered the oldest family of all, and even God did not prevent it.

This story represents the depth of hostility and violence that erupts when expectations are denied, and jealousy over a favored younger sibling festers. On the other hand, Hansel and Gretel, the children of a family in the woodcutting business facing a market downturn, were abandoned by their spineless father (at the suggestion of their wicked stepmother) in the middle of the wilderness. These two siblings stick together in the face of betrayal and death, in a remarkable display of sibling cooperation, using naïve but creative ways—even dropping crumbs along the path—to find their way home.

When they are captured by the wicked witch, who entices them into the local gingerbread house, and is about to put Hansel into the oven to roast him, it is Gretel, the younger sister, who becomes the aggressive one—risking her own safety to shove the witch into the oven instead, and rescue her older brother from certain death.

These two siblings find each other more reliable than their parents. The remarkable ending to the story of this all-time dys-

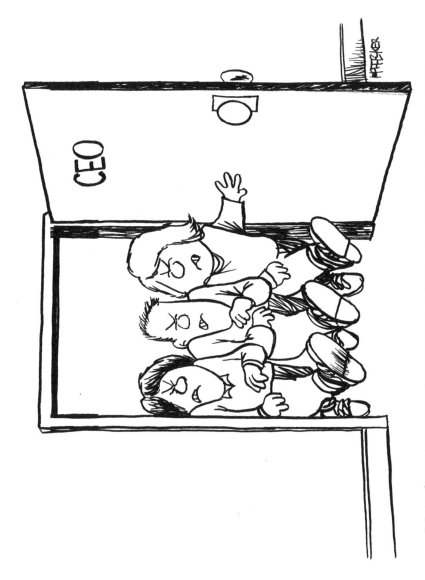

TIP #4. Choosing the Best Candidate Among Siblings Is a Major Challenge for Family Firms

functional family is that the wicked stepmother dies, and Hansel and Gretel return home to their father, who is apparently cleared of all charges of child abuse and neglect, where they happily carry on the family woodcutting business together.

Stories like these which survive generation after generation in the human consciousness usually carry some important grain of truth, or we would not remember them. These two stories represent extreme problems within sibling relationships. Cain and Abel represent the upsetting of the prerogatives of the firstborn, the choice of the unexpected, and subsequent jealousy, murder, and exile. Hansel and Gretel stick together in the face of enormous evil, outwit the wicked witch and their wicked parents, and through collaboration with each other, and their willingness to upset traditional gender roles, live to see a better day. They survive through extraordinary loyalty to their family bonds, even with the father who betrayed them.

TIP #26: SIBLING RELATIONSHIPS ARE THE LONGEST IN OUR LIVES, AND HAVE GREAT POWER WITHIN THE FAMILY FIRM

Both stories tell us that sibling relationships are profound and powerful, not to be taken lightly in the family business. The sibling relationship is usually the longest in our lives: we know them before our spouses, and usually they outlive our parents. The way we learn to relate to our brothers and sisters affects the way we relate in every other social group throughout our lives.

Do I see myself as loved and accepted? Or not quite good enough? Do I see myself as a winner? Or the one who gets more than a fair share of teasing during every family gathering? Have I learned to fight fair? Can I share what is most valuable to me? Or sometimes even let the other go first? Was I the favorite? Or the "black sheep"?

Our answers to these questions are imbedded in those early primary relationships within the family, which gave us our first sense of who we are in relation to others: taller, smarter, smaller, slower, skinnier, funnier, faster. . . . Sometimes those early comparisons get embedded in our brains, and pop up again in the midst of a business meeting, especially if that meeting includes those who still consider someone "the baby" of the family, or don't know that "the baby" will no longer expect to pick the best piece of chocolate out of the box.

TIP #27: MORE THAN 85 PERCENT OF FAMILY FIRMS DO NOT SURVIVE THE THIRD GENERATION

In addition to market forces, natural disasters, and the ordinary life cycle of many products or services, family relationships, especially relationships between siblings and cousins, have a significant impact on the survival of family firms in the third generation.

The founding entrepreneur and his or her spouse ordinarily raise their children with shared faith and shared tragedies, shared chicken pox and birthday cakes, shared kitchen table and shared swing set. When siblings are raised in the same household, by the same parents, with the same work ethic, the same appreciation for fishing or basketball, lasagna or bratwurst, they have a pretty good chance of becoming effective partners in the family firm. After all, they learned long ago how to divide the backseat exactly in half for the trip all the way to Michigan, and how to wrestle one another to the ground without leaving any serious bruises.

But in the third generation, the structure of the family becomes a tad more complicated. As the three offspring of the founding entrepreneur marry and raise their own families, they produce seven or eight sibs or cousins, raised in at least three different households, with half the parents shaped in different families of origin, bringing with them different values, different ethnic and religious traditions, different attitudes toward work and play. Figure 4.1 illustrates the family's interconnection with a genogram.

This capacity of the family to integrate new diversity, new bloodlines, and new customs is central to its enduring generativity; but it makes partnership in business a little more challenging. As the range of differences between people increases, so does the need for building skills to negotiate and resolve conflicts. Working together successfully in an enterprise as challenging as a family firm will require goodwill, good luck, and good work.

In addition, each nuclear family within this three-generation extended family has an eldest child, a youngest child, and sometimes a middle child, which has significant implications for determining who will lead, who will follow, and who will upset the family grocery cart.

TIP #28: BIRTH ORDER OFTEN DEFINES SIBLING RELATIONSHIPS

Birth order has a profound impact on personality development, reports Frank Solloway in his 1996 book, *Born to Rebel: Birth Order, Family Dynamics, and Creative Lives.*[1] Solloway, an MIT researcher on the history of science, compiled a database on more than 6,000 persons, living and dead. In his extensive study, Solloway concluded that eldest children tend to be more conservative, more responsible, and more identified with the parental generation (whom they frequently represented when they acted as baby-sitters). Eldest children are typically high achievers, scoring disproportionately higher on SAT tests than their younger sibs. Since they have a preference for the predictable order, the status quo, they tend to become a little anxious when things get out of control. Their stability and sense of responsibility can be a great asset for a family firm going through treacherous times, when a steady hand is needed.

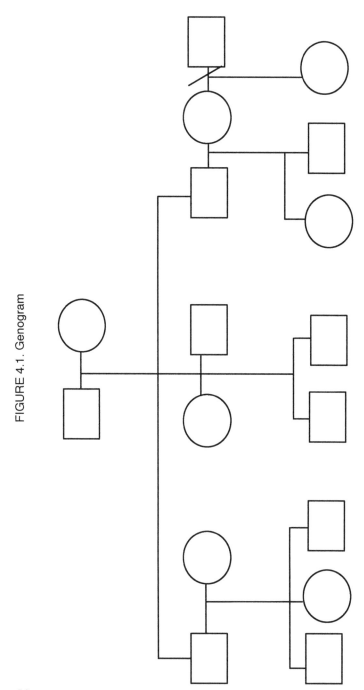

FIGURE 4.1. Genogram

On the other hand, the youngest child, according to Solloway, tends to be more liberal, regardless of social class, more relaxed and willing to explore new opportunities, to take risks to go where his or her elder sibs have never gone—a great asset for the innovative leader of a family firm engaged in a rapidly changing marketplace, where traditional ways of doing business no longer work.

Benjamin Franklin was the youngest son of a youngest son for five generations. After he rebelled against his autocratic older brother, to whom he was indentured as an apprentice in the family printing business, Franklin later became a prime architect of the American Revolution, one of the greatest risks a man of his day could take.

The implication of historical birth order studies for the family firm is that birth order *alone* is not a reliable predictor of successful leadership. The eldest son is not necessarily the most perceptive leader, even though he may have an added dose of responsibility which inclines him to believe he "should" be the leader. Birth order is likely to affect how one perceives problems (let's support the status quo) or responds to them (let's try something new).

TIP #29: MONARCHY WAS REJECTED
BY THE UNITED STATES,
BUT NOT BY ALL FAMILY FIRMS

The United States soundly rejected monarchy in the eighteenth century, and yet some primordial pressure still affects our psyches, telling us that it is right and fitting for the eldest son to inherit the kingdom. Family firms are the only institution in the United States where this feeling persists, with the emotional undertow that can intensify a sense of entitlement or unfairness among siblings.

And even if the family has decided to leave the eighteenth century behind and has named its best possible candidate on the basis of competence and the needs of the company (perhaps the middle daughter), the expectations of the community, the customers, and the suppliers may echo the ancient prerogatives of the eldest son. "How come John didn't become president, and his younger sister did? What happened?" they say quietly to each other, or to John's wife in the supermarket.

> The eldest son, Peter, now CFO, has been groomed since he was six to take over the company. He lies awake all night before the board meeting, worried about last quarter's figures. Finally at dawn, he calls the company's accountant, who also happens to be a firstborn son, conscientious and responsible, and with whom he can share his fears. His younger brother, who shows up nine holes late every sunny morning, discounts his fears, and says he is tired of listening to them, because if this company fails, he has a great idea for starting another one . . .

Firstborn children from different families are often more alike than siblings in the same family. This means that firstborn cousins raised in different households may have more in common than sibs raised in the same household in terms of their feelings of responsibility, their focus on achievement, and their anxiousness with events that spin beyond their control.

These common links between firstborns can be an advantage in a third-generation family firm; they can also become a source of rivalry if each eldest cousin feels entitled to be in charge, and if the family as a whole has never developed clear criteria and a common value base for succession planning.

TIP #30: BIRTH ORDER OUTWEIGHS GENDER AS A DIFFERENTIATING FACTOR IN DEFINING LEADERSHIP STYLES

Birth order has such a powerful impact on personality development ("After all, who got here first?") that *it even outweighs gender* as a differentiating factor. Firstborn women can be as conservative and hard-driving as their firstborn male cousins; a man and a woman who are both later-borns may find common cause in attacking the status quo.

Over time, gender roles assigned by society—girls do the dishes, boys carry out the garbage—have extraordinary power to create different social roles in different sexes. And biology will always be destiny. But it is also true that two siblings of the same gender often develop more divergent interests than two firstborn cousins, one male and one female, born in the same generation with similar family experiences, similar engineering degrees, and similar work histories. As CEOs, the cousins probably will lead the company in similar directions.

Sometimes we meet sibs and say later, "I wonder how those two could be brothers . . ." The blond one became a North Woods fishing guide; the dark-haired one is a concert violinist. With each new birth, the genes are scrambled, in much the way that phone numbers or Social Security numbers are scrambled—with an infinite number of possible combinations. This biological diversity achieved within one nuclear family is an advantage to our species, and an advantage to the family firm. It means that different individuals will bring different skills, different aptitudes to their work in the company. It means that each can develop a complementary niche not only within the family, but also within the family firm.

TIP #31: DEVELOP PRACTICAL STRATEGIES FOR MANAGING RIVALRY IN THE FAMILY FIRM

To develop positive relationships in the family firm, here are some tips:

1. Support the development of the talents of each son or daughter, so that each can develop a unique, positive identity.

2. Let go of old stereotypes and get up to date on the competencies of each family member who seeks employment in the family firm.

3. Develop objective evaluations of each family member employed in the firm through personality testing and observations by nonfamily supervisors, mentors, and responses to frontline experiences.

4. Support the development of a niche that capitalizes on the unique talents of each individual, whether it is warehouse management, sales, or strategic thinking for the whole company, etc.

5. Provide training for family members and/or key employees on healthy ways to resolve conflict, build effective working teams, and make decisions by consensus.

6. Develop your own family's "rules for fair fights," write them down, and ask everyone to implement them.

7. Liberate those siblings or cousins who really don't have the competencies required by the family firm at this time, and support them to find other work or make graceful transitions to a new career.

8. Consider the individual's role in the company when distributing stock. Is the equal distribution of stock to all siblings, whether they work in the company or not, or carry the same responsibilities, always fair?

9. Define the strategic plan for the company first, and then identify the best candidate for leadership to meet those needs, whether within the family or not.

10. Provide opportunities for all family members to get together where the focus is not on the business, and the leadership does not rest with the only sibling who became CEO.

Sibling rivalry is a family issue, born in the backyard trenches of childhood, where the eldest usually is told to "Look out for your younger brother until I get back . . ." or "Give your little sister an extra chance to hit the ball . . . she's only five . . ." And so by countless repetitive patterns of behavior, a family develops a pecking order, an image of who's the organizer, who's the brain, who's usually late, who can get everyone to laugh. When a healthy family grows up, those niches of childhood can be transformed into a new adult family architecture, where all individuals contribute to the unique spaces they share within the family and within the family firm as well.

Succession planning and team building within the company need to be done while you are wearing the business hat and standing firmly inside the business circle. Decision making about hiring, promotion, and succession planning need to be made in the light of the business's public accountability, data, competencies, and adaptation to the marketplace, and with a profound appreciation of the delightful diversity that your family continues to bring into the world, and into the family firm.

Chapter 5

Preparing Your Daughter
to Become CEO

Family firms are predominantly male organizations. Even though U.S. women gained the right to vote in 1920, the monarchical tradition of preference for the male heir has prevailed in the machine shops, construction companies, and meat-packing houses owned by families.

But in the twenty-first century, we are entering a brave new world. The entrepreneurs who built those family firms on sweat equity educated their daughters as well as their sons in the finest schools they could afford, creating aspirations far beyond their own blue-collar origins. And having invested at least $50,000 per daughter in college educations, they are ready to reclaim that investment—if not on the shop floor, at least in the executive offices of the family firm.

A 1994 survey of over 1,000 family business owners by the Massachusetts Life Insurance Company indicated that men still carry more clout than women in family firms.[1] Nevertheless, the survey also showed that women hold proportionately more positions in the top management of family companies than they do in nonfamily businesses. Moreover, women who currently lead family firms are twice as likely as men to envision their daughters taking control in the future (14 percent versus 7 percent).

To take charge of your company, your daughter will need more than a good education. She will need a supportive family, good mentors, on-the-job training, and a motivating dream. There probably isn't one right way to develop leadership potential in the next generation because industries, marketplace requirements, and personalities vary so widely. But parents who identify and nurture the strengths and talents of their daughters as well as their sons from an early age will have better odds of choosing the best possible successor to lead their company into another century, another world.

TIP #32: MESSAGES FROM YOU WILL SHAPE YOUR DAUGHTER'S DREAMS

A growing body of literature about girls' development provides helpful information about how to raise your daughter to become the next CEO. In their 1992 book *Women in Power: The Secrets of Leadership,* Dorothy Cantor and Toni Bernay examined family influences during the childhoods of twenty-five women who were later elected to high political office in the United States during the 1980s.[2] The women interviewed were the first females in either political party to assume roles as senators, governors, or members of Congress for their states or districts. Psychologists Cantor and Bernay cited five powerful messages that these successful female leaders received from their parents in their formative years:

1. You are loved and special.
2. You can do anything you want.
3. It is okay to take risks.
4. You can use and enjoy your creative aggression.
5. You are entitled to dream of greatness.

These women had melted the glass ceiling. When asked how they overcame all the obstacles any candidate faces in the rough game of politics, their common response was, "What obstacles?" They saw formidable obstacles as an ordinary part of getting the job done, a perspective that translates into effective leadership in any business.

The messages that little girls hear can have a profound impact on their success as adults. The women elected to high political office in the 1980s were the first of their generation to create a different kind of dream. They report that their parents clearly played a significant role by listening to their dreams, encouraging them, and giving them space to sharpen the focus of their extraordinary aspirations.

> Abigail Johnson, now in her early thirties, is senior vice president and director of equity for Fidelity Investments, the family firm established by her grandfather in 1947, and now headed by her father, Ned Johnson.

Of course, women enter the marketplace with different biological and hormonal chemistry, but social cues and family communication styles also shape the roles men and women assume in adult life. Carol Gilligan, a Harvard psychologist, argued in *A Different Voice* (Harvard University Press) that when faced with life-altering decisions, women typically think first of the impact on the significant persons in their lives, and second of the impact on themselves.[3] Males in our culture receive much more permission to develop independent, autonomous identities and to make decisions according to their own goals and preferences.

Gilligan's work suggests that males are prepared by countless messages, both spoken and unspoken, to become more independent decision makers, while women may be more collaborative, inclusive, and process-oriented leaders. Most likely, a combination of both sets of qualities is essential for the corporation of the future. The question is, How can both collaborative *and* autonomous leadership be nurtured in your daughter—especially if she is your best or even only potential successor?

TIP #33: SUPPORT THE DEVELOPMENT
OF ALL HER TALENTS

"You can do anything," a successful woman was told. That message is not about foolhardy attempts to fly a plane across the country at age seven, but about testing your daughter's wings in age-appropriate, skill-matched challenges, from soccer to stargazing:

> You can take horseback riding lessons when you're as old as your brother was when he started—six years old . . .

The younger she is, the broader the spectrum of experiences to which your daughter should be exposed: from dinosaur digs to tractor rides, from ballet lessons to stargazing. The sparks of interest she shows will be fanned by parents who support her development, even if she decides to apply to West Point in mechanical engineering, or take her first job in a nonprofit housing development corporation in the inner city.

TIP #34: OFFER SPECIFIC COMPLIMENTS
TO REINFORCE REAL ACCOMPLISHMENTS

In some cultures, notably the Northern European or German, one is expected to do the job right the first time. The adult comments only when a child makes mistakes, and often the parent is harder on his or her own child than on other children, because expectations are higher. False, inflated flattery is useless, if not dangerous, but we do need to catch our children being good more frequently than we catch them being bad.

> I like the way you picked up your toys before we left the house, even before I asked you . . .

TIP #35: ENCOURAGE HER TO TAKE RISKS, ACCORDING TO HER AGE AND SKILLS

The breadth of risk taking is defined within a family. One family I know in the logging business did not consider it risky for an eleven-year-old to climb to the top of a 100-foot hemlock tree and "ride it down" while his father cut through the final wedge in the trunk. In other families, girls and boys aren't allowed to talk with children of other faiths or races because of fear of differences.

The capacity to manage risk varies greatly, even among children raised in the same family. Some sixteen-year-olds have been driving tractors on the family farm for years; another sixteen-year-old getting the keys to a Dodge Viper is a prescription for disaster. Parents who know their children well can calibrate risks according to the child's age, skill, and maturity. They don't "protect" their daughters in ways that limit their future capacity to pursue a realistic challenge.

> If your instructor says you're ready, why don't you ski the black diamond slope this afternoon? The weather looks great today, and I believe you can do it . . .

TIP #36: HELP HER DEFINE REALISTIC GOALS

No matter how medaled a swimmer she is, she will probably never be able to join the Navy SEALS because there are real differences between men and women in large muscle power and stamina. Women are better at fine muscle movements, useful in fields such as needlepoint or brain surgery. Most of the family firms I know no longer require their CEOs to do a lot of heavy lifting, and the most basic tool of business management today—the computer—is sexless.

A young woman of intelligence and confidence can set realistic and extraordinary goals for herself that her grandmother—the one from Eastern Europe who couldn't write English, but who founded a successful dry cleaning chain—could never have fathomed.

> If you want to go to law school, your mother and I will pay your expenses, because your scores on the LSAT were great, and we really believe this is a great opportunity for you and a great investment for our family . . .

TIP #37: GIVE YOUR DAUGHTER EQUAL AIR TIME

Studies of teachers' behavior in classrooms repeatedly indicate that boys are called on more frequently than girls, which means that boys elicit more attention and, it seems, grow in confidence and leadership skills. Parents can make the same mistake. Try a little experiment in your household: keep track for a few nights of how much each of your children talks during dinner. If your daughters participate about as much as your sons—and are listened to without interruption—you are raising potential leaders of both sexes. If they don't get anything close to equal air time, or even equal eye contact, find a way to rebalance the conversations.

> Jennifer, if the presidential election were held tomorrow, who would you vote for?

TIP #38: ASK HER ABOUT HER DREAMS
OF GREATNESS

Little girls used to be limited to four dreams: they could be teachers, nurses, or secretaries, and after they worked for a while, they could become mommies. Now, even after three soccer practices per week, violin lessons, and Advanced Placement Chemistry, girls need time to dream, to create dreams their grandmothers couldn't imagine, among infinite choices.

As Carol Gilligan tells us, young girls' dreams are shaped by the influences around them.[4] Multitalented young women will hide brains behind charm and defer to the boys around them for the sake of maintaining a relationship, or the hope for one. At age eight Jennifer organized the play of all the kids on the block. Will she continue to grow her natural talent for leadership through her teen years? What will happen if she keeps getting the message that it is a turnoff to boys when she tries to lead? Will her dreams die?

Inviting your daughter to try out her wings in the family business through a summer job, or by accompanying you on your next business trip to San Antonio, can introduce her to the world beyond the whims of adolescent boys, and let her know that you take her potential seriously. On a camping trip, a "business lunch" downtown with just the two of you, or a long drive to check out a college, turn off the cell phone and ask her to share her dreams with you:

> What would you like to be doing when you're twenty-five? When you're thirty? What will help you get there? What obstacles will prevent you from getting there?

TIP #39: LET HER KNOW THAT HER CAPACITIES FOR EMPATHY AND CONSENSUS BUILDING ARE VALUED ASSETS

The 1994 Massachusetts Mutual Life Insurance survey affirmed that family firms prefer to reach decisions by consensus.[5] They still want to celebrate Thanksgiving together, with everyone around the table. The feminine predisposition to think of the other first can be a valuable business asset, especially in team building and developing collaborative partnerships. Women have been socialized for centu-

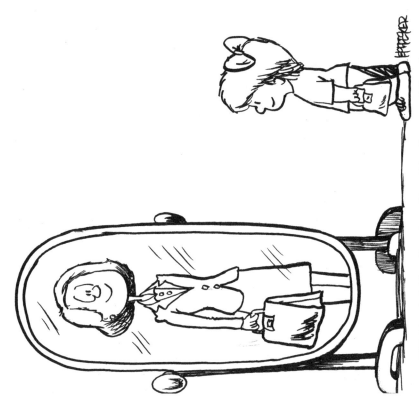

TIP #38. Ask Your Daughter About Her Dreams of Greatness

uries to be empathic, and if they can lace their empathy with timely, creative aggression, the combination can be dynamite. The challenge for top management is to figure out how to utilize these complementary strengths of the daughters who may one day lead the family firm in remarkable new directions.

> Jennifer, why don't you check the Internet for the options for our family vacation, because you already know everyone's schedule, and what each one wants to do. . . .

TIP #40: DURING THE TWENTIETH CENTURY, WOMEN HAVE BECOME A NEW SPECIES

The average life span of women has doubled since the turn of the twentieth century, from forty-two to eighty-something. This change in the life span suggests that women have become virtually a new species. Women who choose to focus on raising children, especially during preschool years, still can have twenty-five to thirty years to contribute to the family firm.

Perhaps that's time enough to become CEO of a major corporation, especially one with her family name on the door. Bright women who bring hard-earned experience as moms managing human resources, budgets, and multiple priorities may find that the jump from the tot lot to the boardroom may not be that far.

> Katherine Graham unexpectedly became publisher of *The Washington Post,* her family's newspaper, following her husband's shocking midlife suicide. She led the paper through the turbulent Watergate revelations and President Nixon's subsequent resignation. By the time she turned the leadership over to her son, the *Post* had become a preeminent national newspaper.[6]

The U.S. Small Business Administration reports that more than one-third of businesses in this country are now owned by women, and that trend will continue to grow.[7] And, remember, those women entrepreneurs are twice as likely as their male counterparts to consider their daughters their successors. Even if your daughter doesn't become CEO, your company may be competing with one of the 36 percent of U.S. companies now headed by women.

The daughters who have come of age since the 1970s expect equal opportunity in sports, scholarships, and stock options. They have emerged from the Saturday-morning mud of soccer fields, as well as from the Harvard Law School, with a perception of themselves that is quite different from the women of previous generations.

TIP #41: THE FAMILY FIRM CAN BECOME A LAB FOR "FAMILY-FRIENDLY" PRACTICES

The family firm can provide a practical laboratory to develop employment policies for women entrepreneurs, such as equal pay for equal work, on-site child care, flexible work schedules for parents with young children or children with aging parents, and generous family leave following a birth or adoption.

Family firm managers may be more motivated than managers in other corporations to provide these "family-friendly" benefits, because their own grandchildren or their own grandparents benefit. By thinking through strategies to utilize the talents of all its members, the family firm will be better positioned to develop the most effective leadership for the future, a central key to the company's survival and success. And perhaps that leader just may happen to be your daughter.

Chapter 6

Partners in Business, Partners in Marriage

A long-married, happy couple was asked what their secret was. "A poor memory" was the wife's immediate answer. If you consider yourself happily married, what would your answer be?

Judith S. Wallerstein, PhD, a family psychologist, recently published a book titled *The Good Marriage: How and Why Love Lasts.*[1] With co-author Sandra Blakeslee, she reported on intensive interviews with fifty couples who identified themselves as happily married for at least ten years.

When both partners also work in the family firm, the challenges to a happy marriage multiply. How do you do demanding work together all day and still spend energy on growing your relationship at home? Or if your spouse is a homemaker, or works elsewhere, how many hours per week do you spend together, sharing something beyond the nuts and bolts of living? How do you prevent an affair before it even becomes a glimmer in the eye?

Entrepreneurs usually succeed because they are highly motivated, focused, and single-minded: "We'll reach one million sales this year—or die doing it!" But the very determination required to succeed in business can block out more subtle emotional cues from a wife or husband that all is not well in the marriage. Benchmarks of success in a marriage aren't quantifiable, like $1 million in annual sales; but failure in a marriage can cost a lot more. It can even destroy a business.

The following are nine essential elements for a happy marriage that Wallerstein recognized in her interviews with the happily married couples. I have adapted her findings to the specific issues that affect partners involved with a family firm. You and your spouse can use these tips as benchmarks to assess your own marriage.

TIP #42: HAPPILY MARRIED COUPLES HAVE SEPARATED FROM THEIR FAMILIES OF ORIGIN

For family members working in family firms, separating from their family of origin may seem preposterous. And besides, perhaps they chose to work in the family firm because they really *enjoy* working closely with family members.

But even if you share a cubicle all day with your brother and have lunch with your father each Wednesday, there are still ways in which you can separate from them as an adult with another life, with a spouse beyond the business. Especially in a family in which the business can swiftly become the center of every conversation, it becomes crucial to define other spaces, other times to clearly shift the center of gravity from the family of origin in which you grew up to the family of adulthood where you are responsible for your own life, your own decision making, your own weekend fun.

Is there a clear boundary between what you share at work and what happens in your intimate life with your spouse? Are there decisions you make that even your brother in the same cubicle doesn't know because they belong within your marriage?

Do you have a social life with your spouse that doesn't involve your extended family? Can you keep fights from home off the shop floor and out of the office? Do you make some decisions—what church you attend, who you vote for, where you vacation, how you manage your money, how you discipline your children—that sometimes differ from your parents' because you and your spouse (who, of course, was raised in a different family of origin) have reached new agreements for yourselves and your children?

TIP #43: HAPPILY MARRIED COUPLES BUILD BOTH TOGETHERNESS AND AUTONOMY

When couples first fall in love they seem to want to be together twenty-four hours a day, seven days a week. They will spend every waking moment together, which means, to go back to our geometry review, their experiences overlap so much that there's hardly space outside the intimate circle they share. This relationship can be illustrated this way:

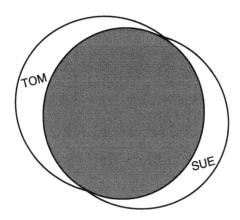

In their long, languid talks they probably dream of what they want their life together to be. As they work through their differences, they may gradually refine a shared vision, full of images of a home in the sunlight and blessed children at play. Because of the energy of new love, they may even be able to put aside the adolescent "I" to create a married "we." They may even develop the profound kind of love in which each of them cares at least as much about the welfare of the other as about his or her own.

The kind of sharing of dreams and realities that builds a steadfast bond between two persons also creates the alternative possibility: because they trust each other deeply, they can also support each other's independence. Beyond the honeymoon, they will seek a new balance, new ways of being autonomous at the same time that they sustain their togetherness. He really does need to play softball two nights a week, and she really does need to work overtime with her new boss, who happens to be a double for Tom Cruise.

And they can trust each other to be autonomous because they both also protect their own sacred time together. They make appointments to be together because they know if it's not scheduled in their planners, it won't happen.

Happily married couples develop enough trust that they can be together and also be separate, dependent as well as independent. How would you draw the circles representing the relationship between you and your spouse today, given the requirements of your work, your family, and your personal needs? What percentage of your time and energy is together? Have the circles become so far apart that you only meet next to a square—the refrigerator? Do you and your partner both agree on the balance you have struck at this stage of your lives between togetherness and autonomy? Several examples are presented below:

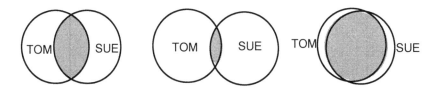

TIP #44: HAPPILY MARRIED COUPLES
BECOME PARENTS

Most couples describe the birth of a child as a deep experience of joy that binds them more completely together. But finding

practical room for a child means negotiating a whole new schedule, especially if both parents are working.

> A Midwestern manufacturing firm took "family values"
> very seriously; they built a nursery onto the back of the
> shop, hired a first-rate child care provider, and invited other
> employees to bring their children as well. Both father and
> mother were then able to monitor the quality of care and
> stop in during the day, even if it was a long one.

"Quality time" is an overrated myth when it comes at the end of
a long workday, with laundry to sort and grass to cut. Kids, especially below the age of five, still do best with a primary caregiver,
preferably a parent who is relaxed enough to drop everything to
play a game and laugh through one more "catastrophe."

A useful norm, even for the busy entrepreneur whose spouse is
able to stay at home with the kids, is to spend at least fifteen
minutes *without interruption* each day with each child, whether
it's a trip to the hardware store or tucking the child in bed at
night. Parents who travel can even tape-record bedtime stories
when they are home, so the children, especially young ones, can
play the tape whenever they wish. Most moms and dads carry
pictures of their children tucked in their wallets, and sometimes
children may want to have a picture of a parent, too, perhaps in a
little plastic frame that will fit right into a small pocket.

But these are small solutions to the child's profound need for
much more parent time than TV time, or sitter time, or even soccer
time. Children whose parents continually put the family business
first often grow up resenting the company, no matter how profitable it will be by the time baseball tournaments and ballet recitals
become dim memories. Time spent with children is invested in the
family's most important asset: the next generation.

TIP #45: HAPPILY MARRIED COUPLES
COPE WITH CRISES TOGETHER

Every couple faces "normal" crises; even the birth of a child is a crisis in the sense that it upsets whatever used to be normal.

Most families also face unpredictable crises that they have to handle together: a diagnosis of leukemia in a child, a bankruptcy, a fire that wipes out a warehouse. Healthy couples develop ways to work together to solve the problem, without blaming each other or even saying, "I told you so." It is not uncommon that divorce follows the untimely death of a child or other major losses because the stress on the marriage intensifies, and the partners have less time and energy to put their relationship first.

Managing stress during a prolonged crisis, such as a terminal illness in a family member, calls for working together to be sure each partner gets the basics: seven to eight hours sleep per night; not too much fast food; a half hour of exercise almost every day; time out together without discussing the latest medical or financial reports; and even a little laughter at their shared predicament. If the couple has a healthy reservoir of trust built up in calmer times, the chances increase that their marriage will not only survive but also become stronger.

Couples who are so stressed during a crisis that they have little time together can keep a journal at their bedside. One can write his or her thoughts and feelings when the other is keeping watch at the hospital or the sandbag line during a flood; the other can respond when he or she has five minutes to spare, even when a relaxed evening together seems like a distant mirage.

TIP #46: HAPPILY MARRIED COUPLES
MAKE A SAFE PLACE FOR RESOLVING CONFLICT

Whenever I meet a couple who say, "We never fight," I get nervous. I don't know how two adults of different genders and genetics, reared by different parents, and having different life-long experiences can possibly agree on everything. *Never* fighting usually is a clue that intimidation has become a way of life, or that conflict gets swallowed and will either express itself internally in ulcers or other medical maladies or eventually erupt with disproportionate force, like a long-dormant volcano.

Anger is a clue to our deepest values. When our core values are violated by deception or betrayal, the healthy response is anger. Even Jesus, who is commonly quoted for saying "Turn the other cheek," sometimes expressed anger vehemently, especially at those who took advantage of the little ones, the poor, or used power to their own advantage. Such anger can be a source of positive energy to change what needs to be changed.

But more commonly, we are stoned by popcorn: the mud-caked shoes in the middle of the kitchen floor during hunting season; no phone call that the meeting will last two hours longer; no gas left in the car for the 6 a.m. trip to the airport.

Some healthy couples have developed rules for fair fights, which they write down during a calm between the storms: no name-calling or put-downs; no problem solving under the influence; no fighting in front of employees. Agreements such as these form a safe corridor so that each partner feels secure enough to disagree before the conflict burrows beneath the surface and builds up enough pressure to blow apart a marriage—and a business.

Confrontation works best when the angry partner first describes what happened, the observable behavior: "You didn't tell me that your sister and her family were coming to visit next week . . ." and then names his or her own feelings: ". . . and I'm angry because you didn't even talk it over with me first." Neither a statement about what has happened nor a statement about one's internal feelings is debatable. The couple can then focus directly on the issue: How do we communicate better about decisions that affect everyone in the household?

Working through conflict by naming the problem, naming feelings, listening to the other side of the story, and developing new understandings or new compromises can *enhance* intimacy. "I didn't tell you because I knew you were getting ready for that big contract, and I didn't want to distract you until that was settled . . ."

The question is not whether a happily married couple ever fights: it's whether their fights focus on the issue and not on putting each other down; whether they follow their own rules for safety during fights; and how soon they can make up. "Don't let the sun go down on your anger," says the Bible, and even clocks that change with daylight savings time and international time zones can't ignore the right time to settle old fights and find new intimacy on the other side of anger.

TIP #47: CREATE TIME AND SPACE
FOR SEX AND ROMANCE

Couples immersed in a family business who are also raising a young family rarely enjoy the leisure that leads to romance. When they do have time to catch a breath, they may be so focused on their own exhaustion or their own agendas that they can't be sensitive to their partners. Discovering the rhythm for romance that is practical for your present life stage and your personalities is crucial. Some couples stay barely connected by spending twenty minutes collapsed in front of the late news together; others plan regular "date" nights, away from the kids and the computer.

A midlife couple who had focused all their energy on their business and their children during the first twenty-four years of their marriage, decided to buy a twenty-four-foot sailboat. They harbor it on a lake within an hour of their home, and spend frequent summer Saturday nights anchored under the stars, with no conference calls or children to interrupt their intimacy. "We would never have made it to our twenty-fifth," they said, "if we hadn't bought the boat—and found new ways to share *No Escape* [the name of their boat] together."

Ironically, the strengths, the looks, and the charm that first attracted your love won't help you sustain the intimacy that enlivens a long marriage. Intimacy means sharing not only your great jokes and great dance moves, but sharing your *weaknesses* as well. Intimacy is letting your partner know you, even when all your jokes are old, and all your clothes are XXLs, and you realize that you are the last in your family to head your company, because it's closing its doors tomorrow. It's sharing not only the wonders, but also the warts, and still being willing to take a risk to please each other, because you are secure enough inside yourself, and in your partner's love, that there is nothing left to hide.

How much of your conversation with your spouse is about the "nuts and bolts" of living, and how much is about personal feelings? How long can you and your spouse last without talking about the kids *or* the business? And even if sailboats make you queasy, what can you do together this week that has a chance of kindling romance?

TIP #48: HAPPILY MARRIED COUPLES SHARE LAUGHTER AND COMMON INTERESTS

At age ninety, Joan Erikson, married to eminent psychologist Eric Erikson for more than sixty years, said that the most important ingredient in a happy marriage is—surprise!—a sense of humor. And Eric Erikson, after a distinguished career at Harvard, insisted that the Chair of Psychology to be named in his honor be called the *Joan and* Eric Erikson Chair, in recognition of her unsalaried but valued contributions to his work. That's partnership.

TIP #47. Create Time and Space for Sex and Romance.

The difference between an "OK" marriage and a good one seems to be that what the couple does together is life-giving, not a burden that takes life away. Happily married couples gain energy from each other, so they keep on doing new and old things together. They can laugh at their own foibles, and even write down time together in their palm pilots, because it's at least as important as picking up dry cleaning, or a check-up with the dentist.

> Sharon and Tom decided their relationship had become routine, and began to try different activities until they found something new they could enjoy together. For example, if Saturday fell on an even-numbered day, Sharon chose a workshop in gourmet cooking, and Tom came along, thumbs and all. When Saturday fell on an odd-numbered day Tom chose a leisurely bicycle ride in the country, and Sharon only fell off the bicycle once. Eventually, they decided that what they really wanted to do was retire within the next five years, and run a bed and breakfast together. Today they serve gourmet breakfasts to hungry bike riders who enjoy the back lanes of the Virginia countryside that surround their new home.

Couples who are willing to take risks together, trying new adventures in which neither is an expert, open up new dimensions of their personalities, and discover new surprises within each other. Much as you might like good times and rich experiences with your spouse to be spontaneous, they won't happen if they're not planned as surely as your business plan, your financial plan, your estate plan. What *is* your marriage plan?

TIP #49: HAPPILY MARRIED COUPLES CREATE AND RE-CREATE A POSITIVE EMOTIONAL BOND

Couples who enjoy great laughs, great times together, and survive fourteen crises may still miss the caring gestures, the awareness of the other's need before it's spoken.

Marital therapists know that there are always three clients in a marriage: the man, the woman, and the relationship. Just as a woman can be described in three or four adjectives as an individual, and a man's personality can be described as well, so too the space between them, the relationship, the unique chemistry they create when their personalities are mixed together, can be described. The same man in a relationship with a different woman experiences a bond with different characteristics, and he himself will be altered by the chemistry that he helps create.

If you've ever walked into someone's kitchen just after a fight, even if you didn't hear the words, you can feel the tension. Although I don't understand the physics of it, I can feel the air tingling with anger, or hostility, or pain. And if you've also walked into a home where there is warmth and love, even if you don't hear any words spoken, you can feel that too. The bond between two married partners can be described as warm, or frigid, or hostile, or brittle, or sexy, or like a cold war. How would you describe the bond between you and your spouse today? How would you like the bond between you to be different than it is?

One person cannot change another, and the divorce courts are littered with those who tried. The only person I can change is myself. I can't even change my own feelings. Sometimes I wish I wasn't as angry as I am; sometimes I wish I didn't love as much as I do; and sometimes I wish I wasn't so bored. Feelings do not have electrical switches to turn them on or off, or even a dimmer switch.

But I can decide to change my behavior: I can decide to get out of bed in the morning; I can decide to speak first after a fight; I can decide to comfort someone who's crying. And if I change my behavior, the other is going to have to do something new as well. That is how the emotional space between a couple is changed. And if I do change my own behavior and speak first, something new will happen to the caliber of my own feelings. And in nurturing the other, I find that I too am nurtured.

TIP #50: PRESERVE A SHARED VISION

In midlife, the future gets shorter. Dreams that young lovers created together can be changed, or lost, or new dreams that would have been unimaginable twenty years before actually begin to take shape. What are the important things you and your spouse have not yet accomplished together? What is the unfinished business in your marriage? How can you put aside the urgent problems to create time for what is really important?

> For years, Nancy had a recurrent dream: she could see herself on a cruise ship, dancing with her husband at the Captain's Ball, wearing a bright red dress. The only problem was that Brian felt awkward on a dance floor, and avoided any suggestion about dancing anywhere. Nancy discovered a woman who offered private dancing lessons for couples in a studio in her home, and Brian, who was competent at everything else he had ever done, agreed to try six lessons. In a private, safe environment he overcame his own self-consciousness, and was able to surprise his wife with cruise tickets for her fiftieth birthday. She wore the red dress.

Nancy, the wife in this vignette, didn't give up her dream, but worked out practical steps to reach it, with sensitivity to her husband's needs for privacy and competence. She was able to invite him to share her dream, and he was able to respond with grace. The dream was realized because each was able to make small behavioral changes, in a way that respected each other's feelings. Both Nancy and Brian then were able to enjoy a terrific cruise, and their marriage is richer today.

The future tells us what the past was about. As you move through your marriage, you may understand in totally different ways why you really chose your spouse, even though at twenty-three you thought you knew. Can you tell her? Can you tell him? Can you share your changing interpretation of the past? Can you share your hopes and fears for the future? Can you look back on your life together with integrity, accepting the truth of your failures as well as your successes?

Necessary Losses, by Judith Viorst, a *New York Times* bestseller,[2] describes a wise perspective on life: that even though our culture and our businesses focus on gain, success, and accomplishment, life is also built on top of losses: the end of childhood, the end of childbearing, the death of a loved one. Paradoxically, the only way I can grow into a new being is by losing who I used to be.

As years pass by, and retirement beckons, letting go of the leadership of the business can be the greatest challenge of all, especially for a successful entrepreneur. "I married him for better or worse, but not for lunch," says his wife, as he tries to define the new chapter of his life. His marriage, even if neglected in the past, becomes a new focus and a new opportunity for growth, even at lunch.

Loss can be the source of new growth in another direction. As an ophthalmologist charts failing eyesight once again, and arthritis distorts your golf swing, the ultimate question is difficult to avoid: what's life all about anyway? Can you share those doubts and fears, that faith and hope with your spouse? Sharing their ultimate vision of life is something that happily married couples do well. My wish for you is that you are among them.

Chapter 7

Not to Decide Is to Decide: Decision Making in the Family Firm

Often the leaders of family firms have been so busy being entrepreneurs that they have never developed the communication and negotiation skills necessary to reach consensus (which is what they really dream will happen at family meetings). They can always get caught in the vortex of the circles—confused about the circumferences of their different and sometimes conflicting responsibilities as family members and/or owners and/or business executives.

At worst, this means that a family firm, while chugging along impressively in the marketplace, may have lots of unfinished business in its internal decision-making process. The buy-sell agreement may have become outdated twenty years ago; there may be growing resentment among out-of-town relatives who feel entitled to superior annual returns; there may be no clear succession plan; and key executives may have to wait until the will of the CEO is read before they know their own futures.

Two brothers in their twenties began a very successful manufacturing company as equal partners. Their boilerplate buy-sell allowed either to buy out the other at book value, using life insurance, in the event that either died. By the time they reached their late fifties, the company had $150 million plus in annual sales, and sons and daughters from both families had begun promising careers within the company. When the elder brother was killed in a plane crash, the younger brother immediately dusted off the thirty-year-old buy-sell, and exercised his legal right to buy his brother's interests in the company at book value, which was, of course, far below its current market value. The eldest son of the eldest brother, then thirty-nine, had been groomed all his life to become the next CEO. "When things calm down at the office, we'll work out a new buy-sell," his father had said to him. Within a week of their father's funeral, he and his siblings found themselves without their fair share of the company, without market-based compensation for the buy-out, without jobs, without a clear legal remedy short of a bitter lawsuit, and with a lot of resentment toward their newly empowered cousins.

In his book, *First Things First,* Stephen Covey writes about the difference between the "urgent" and the "important."[1] Sometimes the urgent blots out the most important decision making of all, which has gigantic long-term consequences for both the business and the family. Reworking an outdated buy-sell is usually perceived as a "not urgent" task, and one that also might upset the status quo or spark smoldering conflict, so this "important" task remains at the bottom of the to-do list, with potentially tragic consequences.

TIP #51: FOCUS ON THE NOT URGENT, BUT IMPORTANT

Who enjoys talking about a buy-sell that is triggered by death, especially when partners know they are no longer in their vigorous twenties? In their 1997 survey, Arthur Andersen reported that a majority of family firms—58 percent—have no up-to-date buy-sell agreements.[2] And that is only one of the significant decisions families in transition need to make.

One practical solution to the family's indecision or avoidance of long-term planning is to create an opportunity for family members to think through their decision making together in a positive, reflective setting. By developing a family forum tailored to the unique needs of your specific family, you can create the solutions, designed in the context of your own unique heritage, that fit your family and prevent conflict, unfairness, and hostility in the future. After all, you don't want half your grandchildren missing from your retirement party.

Although it may seem a little like going to the dentist at first—a necessary and sometimes painful semiannual event—in the long run, like the dentist visit, developing a family forum will *prevent* greater problems, even insidious cancers. And most families I know, along with hard work and new learning, discover new ways to appreciate each other and even have fun together.

TIP #52: DEVELOP A FAMILY FORUM

The family forum is a gathering of all the family "stakeholders" who stand to gain or lose, depending on the success or failure of the company. They meet together annually in a relaxed setting for a weekend, or twice a year, according to the needs of the family, for purposes such as:

- Providing clear information about the goals of the company, so family members can be prepared to support changes, or new strategic initiatives.
- Developing new communication skills as a family, including conflict management or consensus building.
- Building pride in the unique history and values that have shaped this family and this company.
- Learning about the best practices of other family firms, especially on topics such as developing a succession plan, transmitting ownership, etc.

- Developing policies that affect family members directly, such as criteria for being hired in the company, criteria for owning stock, etc.
- Defining the mission of the family and the values that will undergird major future decisions, such as whether to accept a buyout offer.

But, you may say, why open up issues like that? Because the emotional swamp that can engulf a family firm sometimes emerges from forces that lie beneath the surface. Sometimes family members—spouses, in-laws, or siblings who are not employed in the company but whose lives are profoundly affected by the company's policies—perceive forces or threats that day-to-day workers do not. If they have no legitimate forum in which to get correct information, ask questions, and feel that their voices will be heard, they will probably use other strategies—gossip, manipulation, emotional cut-offs, or, at worst, lawsuits—to protect themselves or their own interests. And sometimes the bright son-in-law from Boston does present a terrific idea that opens up a whole new business opportunity for the family firm.

A well-managed family forum provides a sturdy boardwalk above the swamp that family members who work in the company, and those who do not, can walk across together. They can then see both the alligators below them and the sunset beyond them from a similar vantage point.

The family forum provides an opportunity to educate family members about the requirements of the business, to prevent the kind of conflict that can destroy a business. Developing consensus about major issues that concern family members, before they become hot topics, can *enrich* the company, and also the relationships all around the family circle.

Figure 3.2 (p. 40) illustrates the structure one family firm adopted. Their family forum includes all family stakeholders above the age of sixteen. The CEO and the executive team, of course, retain all responsibility for decision making within the business. The family's focus is not to tinker with the management of the business, but to develop policies that affect the family side of the equation.

A consultant who is familiar with family dynamics can manage the flow of discussion and often weave education into the process, so that the family as a whole learns new ways to communicate, to solve problems, to reach consensus, and to develop pride in their own heritage. A skilled, objective consultant can block any one person who attempts to dominate the meeting, and prevent the family from having the same old fight over and over again, while the CEO participates as a family member.

With a well-developed family forum in place, a family can continue to define its interests and control with one voice, even in the event that the best choice for the next CEO is not a family member, or a new consolidator puts an "irresistible" offer on the table.

The Pedersen family, which owns 100 percent of a third-generation Midwestern manufacturing company, is committed to meeting once a year for two to three days, usually at the grandparents' condo in Colorado, during Christmas vacation. All family stakeholders including in-laws, spouses, and grandchildren above the age of sixteen are expected to attend. Family forum meetings are scheduled for two or three days, from 9 a.m. to 1 p.m. The chair of the family forum and its secretary rotate from year to year, so the family experiences other leadership styles and the CEO can enjoy taking an observer's seat. The CEO develops the agenda from the business perspective, and has hired a professional consultant, an expert in family psychology, to facilitate the meeting and provide education as the family develops its own decision-making style, in the light of its own history and values.

Following an afternoon on the ski slopes, the family meets each evening for supper, so that even the kids who are younger than sixteen begin to understand, in a positive way, how important the family business is. The current stockholders usually meet on the third day to take formal votes and discuss legal and financial requirements of any ideas generated by the family's discussion. Each year this family appoints one member to sit on the company's advisory board to represent the family's perspective in discussions along with the accounting, legal, and business perspectives of other advisors.

At last year's meeting, a very bright twenty-year-old grandson, who had previously been primarily interested in golf, announced that, as a result of being part of the family forum, he had discovered that the family firm would be an exciting place for him to work in the future.

TIP #53: DEVELOP A FAMILY STRATEGIC PLAN TO COMPLEMENT THE BUSINESS STRATEGIC PLAN

The best outcome of meeting in a family forum on a regular basis is the development of a written document that encapsulates the family's perspectives on significant issues.

Great-grandpa gave 20 percent of the company's stock to each of his five children, and died peacefully knowing that he had distributed his major asset equally among each of his children, including his daughters. However, after four generations, that stock is scattered across the continent, to descendants whose sole interest in the company is their annual check, while those who have worked hardest to quadruple the company's value now lack majority control. The family members now managing the company have hesitated to expend the capital to buy back the scattered but very valuable stock, and their distant cousins and their lawyers, practicing in four different states, can't agree on a fair market price.

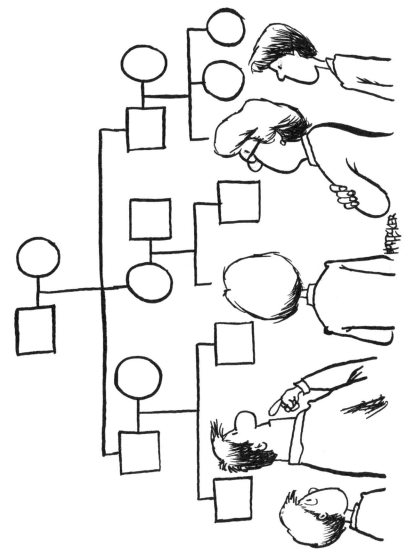

TIP #53. Develop a Family Strategic Plan to Complement the Business Strategic Plan

Sometimes tax consequences become the primary consideration when distributing company stock, for example, in $10,000 annual increments (or whatever number is indexed for inflation in the future) as gifts to the next generation. But thinking through the long-term implications of that choice and learning about other families' best practices might lead to other considerations for its long-term impact on family relationships—and the viability of the business.

> Members of a prolific fifth-generation family decided that only those employed in the company would have the option to purchase stock. Each of the twenty-three members of the fifth generation will have the opportunity to apply for open jobs in the company, if he or she meets the criteria for those specific jobs. Those who choose other careers know they are bypassing the opportunity to own stock in the family firm in the future; they know that they have the family's blessing to choose their own work and their own lifestyles. They also know that, although their parents own real estate and life insurance, there probably will be no other asset in their estates equal to the family firm. Those who choose to work in the family firm can purchase their stock over a five- or ten-year period, leveraged by the company. If the company triples in value during their tenure, and they contributed to that growth, their siblings and cousins will have no future complaint, because they knew the family's policy in advance and made their own choices, often quite happily.

TIP #54: EASY GIFTS AND EASY HIRES CAN LEAD TO HARD TIMES FOR THE FAMILY FIRM

Besides defining criteria for owning company stock, another topic that can be resolved through a family forum as part of the family strategic plan is the criteria for being hired. In the past, many family firms provided safe jobs for any family member who wanted them, no matter what time they showed up for work. In today's competitive business environment, that's a risky decision. It's crossing the boundary from the family circle, where the family accepts its members with all their foibles and limitations, into the business circle, where decisions need to be made on the basis of competency and the rigorous requirements of the marketplace.

By developing criteria for hiring family members in advance, family firm managers, especially in large, multigeneration companies, can sidestep inappropriate feelings of entitlement and pressures to continually pad the payroll pie.

A sixth-generation family with a mature manufacturing company decided on the following criteria for hiring family members:

1. Meet the requirements published in the paper for a specific entry-level job, such as holding an engineering degree, or information systems experience.
2. Demonstrate a good work ethic, that is, show up on time and do a day's work.
3. Meet the same legal and moral requirements as other workers, that is, pass the same drug test as other hires.
4. Demonstrate successful experience in another company, including at least one promotion.

What will work for your company and your family may be quite different than these particular standards; but developing criteria in advance, which even your lovely sixteen-year-old granddaughter knows before she plans her college major, will prevent problems in the future. She can continue to challenge you on the tennis court, but there will be no challenge when her cousin, who met all the criteria, gets hired ahead of her.

TIP #55: DEVELOP A FAMILY MISSION STATEMENT

All of these issues affecting family members, such as who has the privilege of owning stock or who gets hired, fit together under the umbrella of the family's mission, which may or may not be formalized in a mission statement. Companies like Microsoft have mission statements such as, "A computer in every home," which direct their business strategies and operations, and become the standard against which they measure their success or failure.

Families have missions too, as surely as any megafirm, but often their mission isn't written down or defined as a clear commitment for all their members. Sometimes there are disagreements across generations about the family mission, which are played out in action or refusal to act, rather than a clear reassessment of the mission itself. Or sometimes family members make extraordinary sacrifices to fulfill the family's mission.

> The Kennedy family mission to elect one of their sons as president of the United States permeated the life of the family, even in the face of death itself. When the eldest son, Joe, died prematurely in World War II, the next son, Jack, rose to the challenge and did become the president of the United States, despite his relative youth and health problems that caused him chronic pain. After both his elder brothers had been killed, which would have been enough tragedy for most families to assimilate, Robert, the third son, launched his own campaign to "regain" the presidency, which led to his own assassination. Incredibly, the fourth brother, Ted, after the deaths of his three elder brothers, once more stepped into the breach and attempted to present himself as a candidate, even though problems of his own making precluded his nomination.

In the Kennedy family, daughters were apparently exempted from personifying the mission, although apparently they supported its accomplishment according to traditional gender roles. And even though Ted Kennedy has built a lifelong career as a powerful U.S. senator, an eminent accomplishment by most peoples' standards, his political successes are probably considered second best, because they represent a failure to complete his family's unique mission.

Your name is probably not Kennedy, and your family's business may not be securing the presidency of the United States, but this well-known family illustrates the power of a family mission to shape behavior and to determine whether its children see themselves as successes or failures, especially according to the internalized voice of a powerful parent. The family mission can persist in the minds of its grandchildren as the standard against which they judge themselves, long after its initial proponents have died.

TIP #56: RECOGNIZE THE POWER OF YOUR FAMILY'S SAYINGS

Sometimes the mission of a family is expressed in family sayings, such as "Always take care of your brother" (even though he is a late-stage alcoholic who walked out of four treatment programs) or "Every child in this family will be a college graduate" (whether they have learning disabilities or not). Such statements can be a powerful catalyst to action against all odds, or they may have outlived their usefulness. What family sayings affect you or your family? How have they shaped your behavior?

The family forum provides the opportunity to bring the spoken or unspoken mission of the family out onto the table, so that the current members can examine it in the light of their own experience, recommit to its accomplishment, or reconfigure it to more realistic proportions.

The founder of Bosma Machine Tool in Dayton, Ohio, was a teenager in Holland during World War II. When the Nazis came to his front door, searching for the Jews that the family was protecting in the basement, Marinus Bosma outwitted them. After successfully helping their "guests" escape, he spent the rest of the war homeless, moving from place to place with the Dutch underground. When he turned eighteen at the end of the war, he left a devastated Europe behind, joined the Dutch army, and went to Indonesia for yet another adventure. There he met his wife, an Indonesian woman who, as one of thirteen children, had survived the brutal Japanese occupation. After they married, Marinus and Nelly Bosma emigrated to the United States, raised four healthy children, sustained a lifelong marriage, and founded a very successful business. Their family saying, for obvious reasons, is "There's nothing a Bosma cannot do!"

Even if a succeeding generation can never duplicate the heroic acts of the family's founders, they may need to come to terms with their own heritage. What does that family saying mean today? How do I measure myself against it? Would I adapt it in any way in the light of my own adult experience, facing issues my grandfather never faced? And how do those messages from the past shape the mission of my family today?

TIP #57: EACH GENERATION HAS TO REDEFINE THE FAMILY MISSION

In the founding generation, children of entrepreneurs have often found themselves working harder than their peers, sweeping the warehouse floor on Saturday mornings and packing shipments after school during busy season. The mission of the family during the founding generation is to survive until the next bank payment is due and, at the same time, put enough macaroni and cheese on the table for everyone.

As the family firm matures and becomes successful, the mission of the family shifts from surviving to sustaining and, eventually, to transmitting great wealth. The role of children shifts also, from being low-cost helpers to becoming the recipients of great wealth, sometimes without ever pushing a Saturday broom. Raising children with great wealth, while encouraging them to take responsibility for their own accomplishments, is a difficult task.

Families that set limits for their children, and also teach them how to give to others seem to do a good job of preparing their children for great wealth. Princess Diana made specific efforts to take her young princes to visit homeless shelters and hospitals, so they could understand the needs of those who would never enjoy the kind of wealth generated by the Windsor family business. The impact of those visits was probably intensified by their awareness that reaching out to victims of illness and violence was not just a holiday obligation but a priority in their mother's life.

The most influential foundations in the United States were founded by families such as the Fords, the Rockefellers, and the Carnegies, whose descendants redefined their families' missions from acquiring wealth to giving it away.

TIP #58: CONTINUE TO DEFINE CORE VALUES FOR CHILDREN WITH GREAT WEALTH

One of the more simple yet significant messages that Sigmund Freud gave to the twentieth century is that the basis of a healthy personality is the ability "to love and to work." This translates to the capacity to care unselfishly for the good of another and to do something productive with one's own talents. If one of the missions of your family is to raise healthy adults, what do you teach children who have inherited wealth they never earned? How will you transmit values such as love and work to the next generation? How does the family firm, and the wealth it has generated, affect the balance between love and work in your family?

What has the primary mission of your family become? Have you and your family reached consensus on what your family is all about? What legacy do you want to leave?

The following is an outline for developing a family strategic plan that includes items which other family firms have found to be significant. Of course, all of the items may not be pertinent in your situation, or there may be items you want to add. This sample list is intended to prompt discussion and to help you and your family consider alternatives you might not have considered otherwise—to *prevent* a family crisis that is powerful enough to destroy a business.

TIP #59: DISCUSS TOGETHER THE POSSIBLE ELEMENTS OF A STRATEGIC FAMILY PLAN

1. How will leadership be developed in the next generation?

   - Exposure to the business without pressure?
   - The experience of autonomy beyond the company?
   - Assignment of nonfamily mentors?
   - Involvement in the family forum, learning about the business?

2. What criteria will be used to hire family members?

   - Desire?
   - Applying for an open position?
   - Meeting the same criteria as other hires?
   - Exceeding criteria for other hires?
   - Successful experience outside the company?

3. How will family members be compensated?

   - Distributions at the end of the year?

- A fair wage, comparable to the industry?
- The same as other siblings/cousins at the same level?
- A fair base salary plus company/individual incentives?

4. What are the criteria for promoting family members or selecting the next CEO?

- Family or nonfamily member?
- Firstborn male child?
- Competency, based on objective assessments?
- Leadership ability relative to the needs of this company/industry?

5. Is a written succession plan in place?

- Is the buy-sell agreement up to date?
- Does every family member working in the business have a professional growth plan?
- Is every family member preparing a backup person?
- Is the retirement plan of the preceding generation sufficiently funded?
- Who will make the decision about the next CEO?
- What is the best time to select a successor, given the needs of the business?

6. How will stock ownership be transferred?

- By gifting all heirs with equal shares?
- By gifting shares only to family members employed in the firm?
- By allowing family members employed in the firm to purchase stock over time?
- By creating a plan to develop alternate assets for other heirs, such as life insurance or real estate?
- By concentrating majority control in one heir?

7. What will be the structure of our family forum?

- Participation by all stakeholders over the age of sixteen?
- Quarterly, semiannual, or annual meetings?
- Rotating family leadership?
- Introduction of skills and information by a professional facilitator?
- Preference for decision making by consensus?
- What will be the relationship between the family forum and the board of advisors for the business?

8. What is the mission of this family?

- To develop wealth for future generations?
- To preserve the heritage of the family name?
- To provide gainful employment for all family members?
- To support political or religious goals?
- To raise loving and competent adults?

Chapter 8

Standards of Success
in Family Firms

Arthur Andersen's 1997 survey identified the best practices among U.S. family firms:[1]

- They engaged in strategic business planning.
- They had developed active boards of directors.
- Family members were engaged in ongoing education about the best practices of other firms.
- A majority of shares were kept in the family.

In Chapter 3, we also discussed the characteristics of long-lived, successful European family firms, published recently in the *International Herald Tribune:*[2]

- They expressed a strong sense of family history.
- They demonstrated a willingness to employ nonfamily executives.
- Incompetent family members were excluded from employment.
- They sustained family control, especially through self-financing.
- They focused on their basic product range.

These nine characteristics together form an interesting checklist of standards of success against which to evaluate your own family firm. The European firms accentuate a "strong sense of family history," while the Americans emphasize planning for the future. Both recognize the importance of "maintaining family control" through ownership and a focus on the health of the business. Both recognize that the competencies of family members and their capacity to educate themselves about the best business practices of other firms are critical for the survival of the family firm.

TIP #60: WRITE DOWN A LIST OF STANDARDS AGAINST WHICH YOU EVALUATE YOUR FIRM

Certainly family firms come in all shapes and sizes. And standards of success will need to be adapted according to size, industry, and environment. The mom-and-pop motel where you stayed at the beach last weekend probably doesn't have a strategic business plan or a board of directors, even though its owners consider it quite profitable. But the building supply firm, a third-generation company with $7 million in annual sales, where you just bought the lumber for your new deck, probably needs a plan and a board of advisors badly, if they are to survive the relentless pressures on distribution businesses today.

What are the standards against which you judge your own family firm? The eight standards that were common characteristics in successful family firms say nothing about meeting payroll or percentage of profit per year. They refer, rather, to how these businesses operated, especially how they developed clear policies to balance the tension between business and family. They ensure the businesses' continuing success beyond some negative quarterly reports, because the family and the business managers agree on a steady course toward long-term goals.

TIP #61: DEVELOP A BOARD OF ADVISORS TAILORED TO YOUR FAMILY FIRM

One way to keep yourself on a steady course, as you try to define and meet your own standards of success, is to develop a board of advisors, of your own choosing, to support you and your firm in good times and bad. A board of advisors is more than a meeting of a few cronies over some Jack Daniels in December after distribution checks have been handed out. It is an organized group of knowledgeable and trusted experts, whose skills complement yours, and with whom you feel comfortable enough to entrust the secrets of your business, even its actual financial value. Good advisors will tell you the truth, even when you don't want to hear it.

Some family firms include their attorney and their accountant, or other consultants appropriate to their industry, and two or three business leaders—CEOs of noncompeting firms that are perhaps one step ahead of your own in development. Some family firms also include one or two rotating family members, representatives of the family forum, who may not be currently employed in the firm, but who can bring other valuable experience to the table. They also can sustain a sense of family history and an awareness of the family stakeholders' fundamental priorities.

Ideally, for a small firm, the advisory group is no larger than six or seven members, including the CEO. Ordinarily they meet quarterly, with a written agenda and recorded minutes, depending on the current requirements of the business. Larger family firms compensate advisory board members in a formal manner and provide liability insurance. Some CEOs report that organizing their board of advisors, and compensating them appropriately, is the best investment of time and money they ever made. The key is to design an advisory board that fits you and your firm.

With small to midsized family firms, "board of advisors" is the most appropriate title, because its members probably will not hold stock, and the advisors will not have the power to hire or fire the CEO. Ownership and long-term control is retained by family members who presently may or may not have the expertise to offer advice on technical business matters. A board of advisors focuses on "ensuring the business health," even while leaving the ultimate control of the future of the family firm with the family and its appointed CEO.

TIP #62: THE BEST STRATEGY IS TO DEVELOP YOUR OWN STRATEGIC PLAN

Many very successful entrepreneurs in the past had an intuitive sense of how to generate business, and what products or services would sell in their own markets. They never wrote down a business plan in their lives.

But after one more Wal-Mart (a family megafirm) rises from a cornfield on the edge of town, toppling ten or twelve local clothing, shoe, garden, pharmacy, and car repair businesses, today's entrepreneurs seek more sophisticated strategies. Some contract with a professional facilitator to guide them and their executive team through the development of a strategic business plan. Some tap the resources of their local chambers of commerce, which may offer a more economic workshop-type program.

Developing a plan, which probably will need to be updated every eighteen months, forces the company's leaders to analyze their own current performance, and to think "outside the box" of their own past successes. It forces them to analyze their own future potential on the basis of hard numbers. A written plan, which can be shared with family members at the next family forum, can provide a road map to the company's next destination, so family members don't feel like they're bumping along in the back seat, blindfolded and unable to see any turns in the road.

- Does our company have sufficient capital to survive? To grow?
- Does our company have access to the capital to acquire other firms?
- Is our best strategy to search for a "strategic partner"?
- What competitors now challenge our company's growth?

- What needs to happen to take our firm to the next level of development?
- What kind of leadership will be required to lead this company during the next five years? Ten years?
- Are the owners, the family members, and the business leaders prepared to work together to support the firm's future strategy?

Perhaps consolidation will be the inevitable hallmark of family firms in the United States during the twenty-first century, as big box companies continue to gobble up their smaller cousins. Perhaps the most strategic initiative a family firm can pursue is to prepare to sell at the right price, at the right time. But that type of major decision takes us right back into the family circle.

TIP #63: FAMILY ASSETS REMAIN PART OF THE BALANCE SHEET IN ANY MAJOR DECISION

As important as it is to evaluate any major business decision on the basis of the numbers, that is not the whole equation when a family has invested its lifeblood in a company and faces a substantial buyout offer. Even if your most trusted accountant says, "This offer is too good to turn down. It won't be on the table next month . . ." your own sleepless nights may tell you that this kind of decision cannot be reached on the basis of numbers alone.

Whatever decision you reach, whether to sell to a consolidator, to become a bigger box yourselves, to sputter along in indecision, or to cut your losses and shutter the windows, the family voice needs to be heard.

James E. Hughes Jr., in a recent article in *Private Wealth Management* titled "The Family Balance Sheet—A New Way of Assessing Wealth," suggests that "a family measures equity by how well its *family member assets* are thriving . . ."[3] Hughes, an attorney who works with family firms, believes that a family determines whether it is actually preserving its "wealth" by *"measuring the condition of the various family members"* (italics added).

Decision making, then, needs to occur in consideration of the impact, not only on the financial ledger (within the business circle), but also on the primary asset that emerges from the family circle—its members' emotional, physical, spiritual, and psychological well-being.

What intangible value does this business hold for your family members that cannot be contained in numbers? What value does it hold that affects the "condition of the various family members"—a standard of success which other corporations don't have to consider? Sometimes, in a family firm, you paint your future within the numbers, and sometimes, when you consider the meaning the company has for its family members, you paint far beyond the numbers.

Family members will sometimes vote to hold onto a family business even when extraordinary money is on the table, because they have in their minds another standard of success. They want to continue to produce something worthwhile, rather than manage investments in other people's companies for the rest of their lives. Or they want their children to learn how to be producers, not only consumers. Understanding your own family's unique standards of success is important for building consensus on any major decision, and for sleeping well the night *after* you decide whether or not to sign the papers.

TIP #64: DEVELOP A METHOD TO MEASURE FAMILY MEMBER ASSETS

Before your next family forum meeting, ask each family member or stakeholder to fill out a "Family Balance Sheet." Ask them to rank order some specific intangible aspects of being a member

TIP #63. Family Assets Remain Part of the Balance Sheet in Any Major Decision

of a business-owning family (see Figure 8.1). After you have collected all the results, they can be tallied anonymously, or by name, age, and position in relationship to the business, according to the preferences of your family.

After all family stakeholders have completed this form, add the total points assigned to each item together. The items with the *lowest* total points will be the most significant values for your family, with the values most frequently ranked 1 or 2 becoming the whole family's #1 or #2 values. Build a new rank order, based on the combined total for each item from each member. Depending on the size and complexity of your family, you may also want to contrast the differences in ranking between groups, especially between members of the owners' circle, the business circle, and the family circle.

This Family Balance Sheet gives each member of the family, even the shy ones, an opportunity to state the basis for their preferences as a "straw vote," long before they face the pressure of a concrete proposal. The discussion that follows will provide an opportunity to define further the standards on which your particular family wants to base its decisions, especially a decision as significant as keeping the business in the family or selling it.

For instance, if the highest ranked value turns out to be a preference for "the most profitable option," you know that the family as a whole will probably support any effort to seek the highest bidder for a buyout. If, however, items such as, "I enjoy the synergy, the shared excitement we generate as a family," and "I want to continue doing the same kind of work I am doing now" are ranked tops, the family will probably decide not to sell, even if four accountants recommend otherwise. Some things in life may be more valuable than selling to the highest bidder.

Whatever decision the family chooses—whether to sell, consolidate, or sustain its primary business—if you explore the Family Balance Sheet within the circle of the family, perhaps at a family forum, every member will always know that their personal value

FIGURE 8.1. Family Balance Sheet

Directions: Read through all the statements, and then decide how you, as an individual, rank each statement according to its importance to you. Write the number you assign (starting from 1 for the most important value through 13) on the blank at the right of the page. Please do not assign the same rank to any two values.

1. The *autonomy* that comes with owning and managing our own business is very important to me; I don't want to work for anyone else.
   _____

2. I want to retain family *control*, so future generations—even children yet unborn—will have the choice to work in our company and enjoy its benefits.
   _____

3. I believe our work *ethic* should be preserved; I am concerned about the effect of great wealth on children who never earned it.
   _____

4. I believe we should base our decisions on whether family *harmony* will be enhanced.
   _____

5. Good *health* is my primary consideration; I am concerned about the impact of continuing hard work on myself and/or other family members.
   _____

6. I want to preserve the unique *heritage* of this company that our family has worked and sacrificed to build.
   _____

7. It is important to me that our family *name* remain connected to our business.
   _____

8. Our business is a source of great *pride* to me; I want our company to grow into being the dominant player in our market, and perhaps beyond.
   _____

9. I have contributed to the growth of this company in order to make money; we should choose the most *profitable* option, whatever that is.
   _____

10. I enjoy the *synergy,* the shared excitement we generate together as family, working together toward a common goal.
    _____

11. My *time* is very precious to me; there are many other things I want to do in life that will not be possible, if I remain involved in the family firm.
    _____

12. The *work* I do in our company is important to me; in the future I want to continue doing the same kind of work I am doing now.

13. Other value:_____
   _____

---

as an "asset" was given serious consideration. The odds that acrimony or conflict will surface later are greatly reduced. And you will sleep the sleep of the just, knowing that you and your family worked hard to make your best decision, informed by the deepest concerns of all those around the family table.

If a majority does not want to sell in response to an excellent offer, perhaps this signals an opportunity for this generation to consolidate stock among fewer owners. One solution may be to buy out the minority that wishes to redeem their stock at a fair market price. The process of negotiating price and terms needs to be focused not only on the needs of the members, but also on the requirements of the business. Your past efforts to identify the best legal and accounting consultants available will pay off at this juncture. If the process is fair, after the papers are signed, family members may discover a whole new freedom to become family in a new way.

TIP #65: BUILD CONSENSUS TOGETHER, BASED ON YOUR FAMILY MEMBERS' VALUES

Even if everyone wants to work out an ownership strategy together, there may still be wide divergence in the results of the Family Balance Sheet, or a clear division into two or more groups. That is a signal that it's time to call in a skilled facilitator experienced in working with family firms. Then each family member, even the CEO—or the matriarch—can adequately represent his or her own position, and not be responsible for managing the whole meeting. The focus of the discussion remains the value base for this unique family, without the immediate pressure of a specific proposal that requires a response by Monday morning.

If the family is ordinarily cohesive, and they have already worked together on other issues in a family forum, they may want to pursue this discussion themselves. Writing responses on large newsprint paper will provide a common record, and keep the discussion focused. Of course, this process will work best if the family already has agreed on ground rules or norms of common courtesy, such as:

- No interrupting.
- Everyone has a chance for equal airtime.
- Each idea is treated with respect.
- No personal put-downs are used.
- Time limits for beginning and ending the meeting are respected.

TIP #66: THE PROCESS OF BUILDING CONSENSUS CAN BRING THE FAMILY TOGETHER

A process for building consensus follows. First, focus on one value position that received a high rank (such as "we should choose the most profitable option") and then ask the members to look into the future, down the pathway created by that choice:

- What will we each be doing one year from now? In five years? In ten years?
- What will be the impact on our children? Our grandchildren? Our elders?
- How will the family as a whole be affected?
- How will the emotional, physical, spiritual, and psychological well-being of our members be affected?
- How will the company be affected?

Second, focus on the alternate value position (such as "I value autonomy; I don't want to work for anyone else") and ask members to look down the pathway created by that choice, and chart the responses to the same questions:

- What will we each be doing one year from now? In five years? In ten years?
- What will be the impact on our children? Our grandchildren? Our elders?

- How will the family as a whole be affected?
- How will the emotional, physical, spiritual, and psychological well-being of our members be affected?
- How will the company be affected?

Third, take a break for lunch, or overnight, so members can digest the two alternatives and informally discuss together the implications, without pressure on individuals to conform.

Fourth, reconvene, and take another straw vote to see whether a majority is now in agreement on one position or another. If one position seems to be emerging as the primary concern of the majority, explore it further. Try to avoid a vote that could leave a substantial minority in disagreement or pressure the minority to conform.

Fifth, create a chart together similar to the one below. Fill in each quadrant with responses for what the best outcomes or the worst outcomes will be for each choice.

If we *do* choose the most profitable option . . .	If we *don't* choose the most profitable option . . .
What are the best outcomes?	
What are the worst outcomes?	

Sixth, following this discussion (which forces the family members to look at the negative as well as the positive outcomes of each choice), take another straw vote. If a clear majority is emerging, ask each member if he or she can live with the decision and not sabotage it, even if it is not his or her first choice.

Seventh, if there is still substantial disagreement, propose a compromise such as, "We will not accept a buyout offer, even if it is highly profitable, for one year, to allow family members who don't want to work for someone else to develop other opportunities."

Eighth, write down the decision, including any actions that might need to be taken before the family convenes again. For example, the family can agree to authorize the CEO to accept the offer of the highest bidder, if that is the consensus reached within the family forum. If substantial disagreement remains, set a time to revisit the issue, reevaluate the decision, redefine the obstacles, or brainstorm other alternatives.

Ninth, celebrate! Enjoy the experience of knowing that your family, whatever decision was reached, can continue to enjoy each other, and appreciate the assets that each member brings into the circle. You will each know that the decisions you reach regarding your business will continue to enjoy the support of the family, whatever pathway lies ahead.

TIP #67: SOMETIMES, ALL THE KING'S HORSES AND ALL THE KING'S MEN CAN'T PUT THE FAMILY COMPANY TOGETHER AGAIN

Some families, after great effort to work through such a process, with the best consultants they can find, may still disagree. Some members may decide, with the advice of their attorneys, that the price offered in a buyout is not fair, and their best alternative is a lawsuit, a last resort. I have known families that have suffered the repercussions of hostile lawsuits for generations; I have also known one family where a lawsuit became an opportunity for new self-definition, and freedom from an enmeshed, dysfunctional family system that needed to be broken before anyone could be healed.

TIP #68: AT THE END OF LIFE, RECOGNIZE YOUR OWN CAPACITY FOR LOVE AND WORK, AND THE WAYS YOUR FAMILY AND YOUR BUSINESS HAVE ENRICHED EACH OTHER

The way you and your family determine whether you are successful depends on your grandparents' dreams—and how far you have come from where they started. Success also depends on your own inner journey, as you define through the progressive decades of your life what gives meaning to your work, and energy to your capacity to love.

The way you define success in your twenties differs greatly from the way you define it in your eighties, and the journey itself, between those two periods in life, is perhaps more important than any other concrete outcome you can measure. The ultimate standard of success may not be your net worth, or even the value of your company. It may be your capacity to love and to be loved.

At the end of life, most people don't say, "I wish I had worked more . . . ." What most people cherish is their loved ones, the relationships that have given meaning to their lives, usually their families, and the spiritual significance they have given to the good work they have done. "To love and to work" is not a bad formula for a healthy, creative life. These two essential dimensions of life are powerfully expressed in the family and in the business. And the successful ones are those who live to enjoy them both, knowing how each can enrich the other.

References

Chapter 1

1. Massachusetts Mutual Life Insurance Company (1994). *1994 Research Findings: A Telephone Survey of 1002 Family Business Owners.* Springfield, MA.

Chapter 3

1. Tagiuri, Renate and Davis, John A. (1982). "Bivalent Attributes of the Family Firm," Working Paper, Harvard Business School, Cambridge, MA. Reprinted (1996) *Family Business Review* IX (2), 199-208.

2. Wall, Barbara (1997). "Through Market Slumps and Takeover Wars, How the Oldest Firms Survive." *International Herald Tribune,* March 22, p. 15.

3. Nager, Ross W., Beaudoin, Aronoff, Craig E., and Ward, John L. (1997). *Arthur Andersen/Mass Mutual American Family Business Survey.* Chicago: Kennesaw State University and Loyola University. Arthur Andersen Center for Family Business.

4. Pozo, Ernesto (1989). *Smart Growth: Critical Choices for Business Continuity and Prosperity.* San Francisco: Jossey-Bass.

Chapter 4

1. Solloway, Frank J. (1996). *Born to Rebel: Birth Order, Family Dynamics and Creative Lives.* New York: Pantheon Books.

Chapter 5

1. Massachusetts Mutual Life Insurance Company (1994). *Research Findings: Telephone Survey of 1002 Family Business Owners.* Springfield, MA.

2. Cantor, Dorothy W. and Bernay, Toni (1992). *Women in Power: The Secrets of Leadership.* Boston: Houghton Mifflin.

3. Gilligan, Carol (1982). *In a Different Voice.* Cambridge, MA: Harvard University Press.

4. Ibid.

5. Massachusetts Mutual Life Insurance Company (1994). *Research Findings: Telephone Survey of 1002 Family Business Owners.* Springfield, MA.

6. Graham, Katherine (1997). *Personal History.* New York: Knopf.

7. U.S. Small Business Administration Office of Advocacy, Dr. Bruce D. Phillips, director, and Alicia Robb, economist (October, 1998). "Women in Business: A Report on Statistical Information About Women-Owned Businesses." Washington, DC: U.S. Small Business Administration. See also www.sba.gov/ADVO/.

Chapter 6

1. Wallerstein, Judith and Blakeslee, Sandra (1995). *The Good Marriage: How and Why Love Lasts.* New York: Warner Books.

2. Viorst, Judith (1986). *Necessary Losses.* New York: Simon & Schuster.

Chapter 7

1. Covey, Stephen R., Merrill, A. Roger, and Merrill, Rebecca R. (1994). *First Things First.* New York: Simon & Schuster.

2. Nager, Ross W., Beaudoin, Lara, Aronoff, Craig E., and Ward, John L. (1997). *Arthur Andersen/Mass Mutual American Family Business Survey.*

Chapter 8

1. Nager, Ross W., Beaudoin, Lara, Aronoff, Craig E., and Ward, John L. (1997). *Arthur Andersen/Mass Mutual American Family Business Survey.* Springfield, MA.

2. Wall, Barbara (1997). "Through Market Slumps and Takeover Wars, How the Oldest Firms Survive."

3. Hughes, James E. Jr. (1997/1998). "The Family Balance Sheet—A New Way of Assessing Wealth," *Private Wealth Management,* pp. 58-59.

RESOURCES FOR FURTHER READING

Stories of Prominent American Family Firms

Crown, Judith and Coleman, Glen (1996). *No Hands: The Rise and Fall of the Schwinn Bicycle Company, an American Institution.* New York: Henry Holt and Company.

Pottker, Jan (1995). *Crisis in Candyland: Melting the Chocolate Shell of the Mars Family Empire.* Bethesda, MD: National Press Books.

Tifft, Susan E. and Jones, Alex S. (1991). *The Patriarch: The Rise and Fall of the Bingham Dynasty.* New York: Summit Books, Simon & Schuster.

Further Reading in Human Behavior

Carter, Elisabeth and McGoldrick, Monica, eds. (1988). *The Changing Family Life Cycle: A Framework for Family Therapy.* New York: Gardner Press.

Covey, Stephen R., Merrill, A. Roger, and Merrill, Rebecca R. (1994). *First Things First.* New York: Fireside, Simon & Schuster.

Green, Robert Jay and Framo, James L., eds. (1981). *Family Therapy: Major Contributions.* New York: International Universities Press, Inc.

Kaslow, Florence W. and Schwartz, Lita Linzer (1997). *Painful Partings: Divorce and Its Aftermath.* New York: John Wiley & Sons.

Levinson, Daniel J. (1996). *Seasons of a Woman's Life.* New York: Knopf.

Real, Terrence (1997). *I Don't Want to Talk About It: Overcoming the Secret Legacy of Male Depression.* New York: Fireside, Simon & Schuster.

Scarf, Maggie (1995). *Intimate Worlds: Life Inside the Family.* New York: Random House.

Viorst, Judith (1986). *Necessary Losses: The Loves, Illusions, Dependencies and Impossible Expectations That All of Us Have to Give Up in Order to Grow.* New York: Simon & Schuster.

Whitesides, Mary with Aronoff, Craig E. and Ward, John L. (1993). *How Families Work.* Marietta, GA: Business Owners Resources.

Further Reading About Managing Family Businesses

Astrachan, Joseph H., ed. (1988f.). *Family Business Review: Journal of the Family Firm Institute.* Boston.

Bork, David (1993). *Family Business, Risky Business: How to Make it Work.* Aspen, CO: Bork Institute for Family Business.

Danco, Leon A. (1975). *Beyond Survival: A Business Owner's Guide for Success.* Cleveland: University Press.

Gersick, Kelin, Davis, John A., Hampton, Marion McCollom, and Lansberg, Ivan. (1997). *Generation to Generation: Life Cycles of the Family Business.* Boston: Harvard Business School Press.

Jaffe, Dennis, T. (1990). *Working with the Ones You Love: Conflict Resolution and Problem-Solving Strategies for a Successful Family Business.* Berkeley, CA: Conari Press.

Muson, Howard, ed. *Family Business Magazine.* Philadelphia.

Ward, John (1987). *Keeping the Family Business Healthy: How to Plan for Continuing Growth, Profitability, and Family Leadership.* San Francisco: Jossey-Bass.

For Product Safety Concerns and Information please contact our EU representative GPSR@taylorandfrancis.com Taylor & Francis Verlag GmbH, Kaufingerstraße 24, 80331 München, Germany

Batch number: 08153797

Printed by Printforce, the Netherlands